TEAM 5 Together

Activity Book

T0373460

Contents

Pearson

Starter The WOW! Team

1 **Write the names of the WOW! Team. Then read and complete.**

> four   fun   ideas   ~~magazine~~   people   read   team   write

A   B   C   D

1 **Lara:** WOW! or World of Wonder! is our online ___magazine___. We think it's _____!

2 **Bobby:** There are _____ of us on the WOW! _____. We enjoy working together!

3 **Arlo:** We _____ about lots of different topics that are interesting for young _____.

4 **Ting:** Do you have any _____ for our magazine? Tell us what you want to _____ about!

2 **Match the two parts of the dialogues. Which units are they about?**

1 Do you like playing team sports after school?

2 Do you usually do your homework on a computer?

3 Do you want to go to the museum with me today?

4 How many people are there in your family?

5 Let's go to the shopping centre this afternoon.

6 I really enjoy spending time in the mountains.

7 What TV programmes do you enjoy watching?

8 Do you and your friends like watching plays at the theatre?

9 I'm going to New York with my parents next month.

a OK. I need new clothes for school.

b Sure! I love learning about history.

c No, we prefer watching films at the cinema.

d I do too! I love hiking and camping.

e I'm really keen on talent shows.

f Yes, I do. I'm in the basketball team.

g Wow! You and your family travel a lot!

h Yes, I do. I use my parents' laptop.

i Four. My parents, my sister and me!

3 **Which three topics from Activity 2 do you think are the most interesting? Why? Write.**

1 _____

2 _____

3 _____

1 **Read and circle the correct words.**

1 Arlo has **curly** / **straight** hair. It's brown.
2 Lara's hair is **short** / **long** and quite dark.
3 Bobby has **fair** / **dark** hair. It's very short.
4 Ting's hair is black. It's **curly** / **straight**.
5 Arlo says that he's **good** / **bad** at sports.
6 Lara's pretty and she has **green** / **brown** eyes.
7 Bobby isn't tall. He's **short** / **medium-height**.
8 Ting says that she's **bossy** / **friendly**.

2 **Read the descriptions and write the adjectives.**

brave   chatty   energetic   ~~friendly~~   pretty   noisy

1 We love meeting new people. We're _friendly_.
2 I'm not afraid of anything. I'm _____.
3 He's always busy and never tired. He's _____.
4 She has a very nice face. She's _____.
5 I want to sleep. Please don't be _____.
6 Those students talk a lot. They're very _____.

3 **Read and complete the adjectives.**

1 We enjoy sports that are f_un_____.
2 Tom has a very nice face. He's h_____.
3 I'm very good at Maths problems. I'm c_____.
4 You always help people. You're very k_____.
5 He always tells me what to do. He's b_____.
6 I love making things. I'm very c_____.

4 **Complete the sentences about you and your partner. Then compare your answers.**

About me	About my partner
I have _____.	My friend has _____.
I'm _____ and _____.	My friend is _____ and _____.
I'm also _____.	He's / She's also _____.
I'm not _____.	My friend isn't _____.

Free-time fun

Vocabulary

1 **Read and circle the correct words.**

1 We sometimes **play** / **go** / **do** skiing in the mountains.
2 My brother and I often **play** / **go** / **do** table tennis at home.
3 Emma and her mother often **play** / **go** / **do** yoga together.
4 My friends and I don't **play** / **go** / **do** badminton very often.
5 I don't **play** / **go** / **do** athletics in the summer. It's too hot!
6 Many people **play** / **go** / **do** ice skating in the winter.

2 **Look at the pictures. Read and complete the messages.**

What do you do in your free time?

| Tom | I usually ¹ _play hockey_ after school. At weekends, I ² _____ with friends. |

| Ana | I ³ _____ on the school team. It's fun! I also ⁴ _____ . It's my favourite sport. |

| Kevin | I ⁵ _____ with my friends in the winter. In the summer, we ⁶ _____ every day. |

3 💡 **Read the *I'm learning* box. Complete the lists with sports from Pupil's Book page 9. Then add more sports you know.**

I'm learning

Making lists
Making lists can help you learn and remember new words. For example, you can make lists of sports with *play*, *go* and *do*.

play	go	do
football		

4 💡 **Write five sentences about your favourite sports.**

WOW! Team Talk 1

1 (1.4) **Read and complete the sentences from the dialogue on Pupil's Book page 10. Then listen and check.**

1 What _____*are you*_____ doing, Lara?
2 _____ really do all those sports?
3 Well, I go _____ every day.
4 _____ do you go snowboarding?
5 I _____ go snowboarding indoors.
6 I'm learning to ski, but I _____ very often.

2 **Write the dialogue on Pupil's Book page 10 again and answer the questions. Write complete sentences.**

1 What team sports does Arlo play? *Arlo plays basketball and volleyball.*
2 Why does Arlo go scooting every day? _____
3 When does Lara go cycling? _____
4 How often does Lara do gymnastics? _____

3 **Order the words to make questions. Then write true answers for you.**

1 you What doing now are *What are you doing now? I'm …*
2 sports do What do you _____
3 often you go do cycling How _____
4 you Do often scooting go _____

4 (1.5) **Read and complete the dialogues with the correct expressions. Then listen and check.**

I don't believe it! | ~~Really?~~ | You're so funny! | Really?

1 A: I don't like basketball.
  B: ___*Really?*___ It's my favourite sport.

2 A: I'm going skiing tomorrow.
  B: _____ That's great!
  A: Yes. Why don't you come, too?

3 A: I do athletics every day after school.
  B: _____ You hate running.
  A: Not any more. I want to stay healthy.

4 A: Look! I can walk like a penguin!
  B: _____

5 **Work in pairs. Write another dialogue for each expression. Then act out the dialogues.**

Present simple and Present continuous

1 🎧 (1.8) **Listen and complete the sentences. Use the Present simple or Present continuous.**

1 Emily ___is talking to___ Adam at the moment.

2 Emily _____ with Molly right now.

3 Emily _____ on Tuesdays.

4 Adam _____ every day.

5 Danny always _____ after school.

2 <u>Underline</u> **the mistakes and write the correct sentences.**

1 I <u>read</u> a new mystery novel at the moment.

   I'm reading a new mystery novel at the moment.

2 We're playing football twice a week.

   _____

3 Are you going swimming often in the summer?

   _____

4 Does Suzy wear blue jeans today?

   _____

5 He isn't doing any sport on Mondays.

   _____

6 They don't cycle because it's raining.

   _____

3 **Read and complete the sentences. Use the Present simple or Present continuous.**

1 Emma ___is talking___ (talk) with her friend Ana at the moment.

2 My friends and I _____ (not/go) skiing very often.

3 _____ Mark _____ (do) his homework right now.

4 I sometimes _____ (play) table tennis with my brother.

5 _____ your parents _____ (go) to rock concerts?

6 You _____ (not/wear) your sports clothes now.

4 **Make Present simple or Present continuous questions. Then write true answers for you.**

1 what / sports / you / like
   What sports do you like? I like …

2 what / you / wear / today
   _____

3 you / watch / TV / now
   _____

4 your / teacher / speak / English
   _____

5 it / rain / at the moment
   _____

5 💬 **Work with your partner. Ask them your questions from Activity 4 and write their answers.**

   _____
   _____
   _____
   _____

》》 Grammar reference, page 118

 **Book Club**

1 `After you read` **Read the story on Pupil's Book page 12 again. Who says these lines? Write.**

1 ___Mum___ Why don't you practise playing the piano?

2 _____ Hmmm, no. I prefer dancing.

3 _____ I'll just play some computer games or watch cartoons.

4 _____ It's time to play the music. It's time to sing our songs.

5 _____ What are you all doing? I'm bored.

6 _____ We have no Wi-Fi. I heard music from next door.

2 **Read and number the events in the story from 1 to 6.**

a ___ Roly says that he doesn't like singing.

b ___ It's raining and then there's no Wi-Fi.

c ___ Mo is creative so he makes the invitations.

d _1_ Flora feels bored because it's raining outside.

e ___ A lot of people come to see the concert.

f ___ Flora is playing the piano when Pip comes in.

3 **Read the sentences and circle _T_ (true) or _F_ (false). Explain your answers.**

1 Flora wants to practise playing the piano. **T /(F)** _She says that she hates playing the piano._

2 Flora doesn't want to do a puzzle. **T / F** _____

3 Pip can't sing, but she can play a musical instrument. **T / F** _____

4 Roly doesn't like singing, but he likes dancing. **T / F** _____

5 Mo wants to sing and dance in the show. **T / F** _____

6 The concert finishes at 7 o'clock in the evening. **T / F** _____

4 **Read the _Work with words_ box. Write the questions. Then write true answers for you.**

Work with words

_do_ + noun
We use the verb _do_ in some expressions with nouns.

I **do homework** in the evening.
We **do athletics** in PE.

1 you / a lot of homework?
   Do you do a lot of homework?
   Yes, I do.

2 your mum / Sudoku puzzles?
   _____
   _____

3 you / athletics / after school?
   _____
   _____

4 your friends / gymnastics?
   _____
   _____

5 💡 **Write sentences about you and your friends and family. Use expressions with _do_.**

Vocabulary and Grammar

1 🎧 **(1.12) Complete the hobbies. Then listen and number them in order.**

a
d o_ p u z z l e s

b
_ _ k _ v _ d _ _ _ _

c
_ r _ t _ _ _ _ a _ y   `1`

d
p _ _ _ m _ s _ _ _ l
_ ns _ _ _ m _ _ _ s

e
_ o _ _ _ c _
c _ _ _ s

f
_ _
p _ _ _ o _ _ _ ph _

2 **Read and complete the sentences.**

1 I like putting on ___shows___ . I want to be an actor!

2 My sister is really into pop music, so she often goes to _____ .

3 My friends and I watch _____ . Our favourites are about superheroes.

4 My grandparents do _____ in their free time. They have lots of plants.

5 I enjoy making _____ of cars and aeroplanes.

6 People say I'm a good singer. I sing in a _____ twice a week.

State verbs

3 **Look, read and complete the sentences with affirmative or negative state verbs.**

love   like   hate   prefer

1 He ___loves___ making models in his bedroom.

2 They _____ doing the gardening at the weekends.

3 She _____ watching cartoons on Saturdays.

4 She _____ singing after school.

5 They _____ making videos in their free time.

6 He _____ singing in a choir. It isn't fun for him.

4 💡 **Write about yourself. Use hobbies from this lesson and your own ideas. Then compare with your partner.**

1 I like _____ and _____ .

2 I don't like _____ and I hate _____ . I prefer _____ .

3 I love _____ . It's great!

Grammar reference, page 118

WOW! Culture ①

1 **After you read** **Read the text on Pupil's Book page 14 again. Then complete the sentences.**

1 Lots of people like _____ and watching ___*rugby*___ in New Zealand.

2 There is a special kind of _____ for _____ called Rippa Rugby.

3 In _____, there's an important music _____ called *Eisteddfod*.

4 Welsh people _____ songs and write _____ to celebrate *Eisteddfod*.

5 Cross-country _____ is popular in _____ countries, like Canada.

6 Some people _____ enjoy cross-country skiing.
They prefer _____ skiing.

2 **Answer the questions. Write complete sentences.**

1 Why must rugby players be careful?

It can be dangerous. _____

2 What is unusual about how children play Rippa Rugby?

_____

3 How do many people in Wales practise their singing?

_____

4 Where do people celebrate *Eisteddfod* in Wales?

_____

5 Why is cross-country skiing good for your body?

_____

6 What weather is good for cross-country skiing?

_____

3 (1.14) **Listen and complete the sports review.**

Golf is an ¹ ___*outdoor*___ sport that people ² _____ all around the world. A lot of people ³ _____ playing it. Golf is a game that comes from ⁴ _____ and it is about ⁵ _____ years old. There are ⁶ _____ of golf courses in Scotland today. The oldest golf competition in the UK is the ⁷ _____ Open, which takes place in ⁸ _____ every year.

4 📶 **Choose one of the sports in the box or another sport. Use the internet to find answers to the questions. Share your ideas with the class.**

> lacrosse in Canada   baseball in the USA   netball in Australia   golf in Scotland

1 What kind of sport is it?

2 Who plays or watches the sport?

3 What equipment do players need?

4 What is interesting about the sport?

5 Why do people enjoy playing or watching it?

English in action
Making and responding to suggestions

1 (1.17) **Match sentences 1–6 to answers a–f. Write. Then listen and check.**

> **a** No, I don't think so. I don't like team sports.
> **b** ~~Yes, I can. But I already play the guitar.~~
> **c** What's that?
>
> **d** That's a good idea.
> **e** That sounds good! When is it?

Girl: Why don't you sing in the school choir? Can you sing?

Boy: ¹ *b Yes, I can. But I already play the guitar.* _____

Girl: You could play hockey.

Boy: ² _____

Girl: OK. How about going to the video club at school?

Boy: ³ _____

Girl: It's a club where you learn to make videos.

Boy: ⁴ _____

Girl: It's at half past three on Wednesdays. You could go this week!

Boy: ⁵ _____

2 ✷ **Read the dialogues. Write suggestions. Then act out the dialogues with your partner.**

1 A: I'm bored and there's nothing on TV.

   B: Why don't you _____ ?

2 A: I want to learn a new sport.

   B: How about _____ ?

3 A: I don't know what to do this weekend.

   B: You could _____ .

4 A: I need a new hobby.

   B: Why don't you _____ ?

5 A: I don't have many friends at school.

   B: You could _____ .

Pronunciation

3 💬 (1.18) **Listen and circle** (can) **if it's stressed and underline** *can* **if it isn't stressed. Then practise with your partner.**

A: I'm bored. I don't know what to do.

B: Hmm. I have a good idea. I can play the piano. Can you?

A: No, I can't play the piano, but I can sing.

B: OK, great. And can you dance?

A: Yes, I can.

B: I can dance, too. Let's put on a show!

A: That's a good idea.

Literacy: interviews

Reading

Words in context

1 **Read the definitions and write the words.**

freedom   altitude   ~~oxygen~~   energy   hostel   route

1 a gas in the air that living things need _____oxygen_____

2 a simple, cheap place to sleep _____

3 physical power that we use to do things _____

4 the line or way from one place to another _____

5 the ability to do what you want in your life _____

6 the height of a place or thing _____

2 **Read the text on Pupil's Book page 16 again. Then read the sentences and write T (true), F (false) or DS (doesn't say). Explain your answers.**

1 Helen doesn't enjoy short cycling trips.

   [DS] _They only mention long cycling trips they enjoy._

2 They're planning a long trip from Chile to Argentina.

   ☐ _____

3 Helen and Rob aren't using their tent at the moment.

   ☐ _____

4 Rob is writing a blog post and some emails right now.

   ☐ _____

5 They did a very a long cycling trip ten years ago.

   ☐ _____

6 Next year, they want to cycle across North America.

   ☐ _____

3 **Read the sentences. Which questions from the interview do they help answer? Write.**

1 Sometimes we have video chats with our friends and family. _____Question 5_____

2 We have to stop and rest more often at those altitudes. _____

3 Rob wants to visit China and cycle along the Great Wall. _____

4 Last year we cycled across five countries in Europe. _____

5 We always have lots of chocolate in our backpacks. _____

6 Our best friends are people we met on cycling trips. _____

7 We also have sleeping bags to keep us warm! _____

4 **Plan a long a cycling trip in your own country. Discuss the questions and make notes. Then share your ideas with the class.**

1 Where are you going to start and finish?

2 How long are you going to be away?

3 Where are you going to sleep?

4 What are you going to do in the evenings?

5 What equipment do you need for your trip?

6 Do you want to write a blog about your trip?

Writing

1 **Read and write the correct sentences. Use contractions.**

1 I am learning to ski. It is difficult, but that does not stop me!

I'm learning to ski. It's difficult, but that doesn't stop me!

2 Kate and Susan do not like yoga. They say it is boring. They are keen on judo.

_____

3 We have football practice today. There is a match on Saturday. It is the final game.

_____

4 Sam is good at basketball, but he is not the best player on the team. That is me!

_____

5 I do not make models. They are expensive and I don't have a lot of money.

_____

6 My friends are not keen on sports, but that is OK. They have other interests.

_____

> **tip Writing**
>
> Make sure you form contractions correctly:
> _it is = it's_
> _I have = I've_
> _does not = doesn't_
> _she is = she's_

2 **Write some questions for an interview about a sport.**

Include lots of question words, e.g. _What is your favourite sport? When do you usually play this sport?_

Ask questions, e.g. _What is the best thing about this sport? Where is the most interesting place you can play this sport?_

Write questions that will find out interesting information, e.g. _When did you start playing this sport? What do you have to wear to play this sport?_

3 **Now write your interview questions.**

4 **Check your work. Tick (✓) the steps you have done.**

Have I included lots of question words? ☐

Have I asked questions using _the best, the most interesting_, etc.? ☐

Have I asked questions to find out interesting information? ☐

Have I used contractions correctly? ☐

1 **Complete the phrases for sports and hobbies.**

1   c_ollect_ _cards_

2   d____ _____

3   d____ ____ _____

4   g_____ _____

5   g_____ _____

6   m_____ _____

7   p_____ _____

8   w_____ _____

2 **Write sentences in the Present simple or Present continuous.**

1 Mark / not / play football / now

_____

2 you / study / French / every week / ?

_____

3 my / parents / eat / sandwiches / lunch / every day

_____

4 I / watch / film / at the moment

_____

5 Nina / do / yoga / right now / ?

_____

6 we / not wear / shorts / at the weekend

_____

3 **Write about your free-time activities. Compare with your partner.**

1 I often _____ after school.

2 I sometimes _____ in the evening.

3 I'm taking _____ lessons at the moment.

4 I love _____ at the weekend.

5 I don't like _____ in my free time.

6 I enjoy _____ with my friends.

Self-evaluation

4 **Answer the questions about your work in Unit 1.**

1 How was your work in this unit? Choose.   ☐ OK   ☐ Good   ☐ Excellent

2 Which lesson was your favourite? _____

3 Which parts of the unit were difficult for you? _____

4 What new things can you talk about now? _____

Get ready for...

Think! 1 Read the task carefully. Make sure you know what you have to do.

Try! 2 🎧 **1.20** Look at the picture. Which girl is Katy? Listen and tick (✓).

Do! 3 🎯 🎧 **1.21** Listen and draw lines.

> **tip** Exam
> Read the names on the page before you start. Then listen for the names.

Holly   Sophia   George

Richard   Michael   William   Emma

A2 Flyers Reading and Writing Part 1

Think! **1** Read the task carefully. Make sure you know what you have to do.

Try! **2** Read the definitions. Choose the correct words.

1 It's an indoor sport that we play in teams. **A** athletics **B** (volleyball) **C** skiing

2 These are special days when we have celebrations. **A** parties **B** concerts **C** festivals

3 It's a book where people write their ideas. **A** diary **B** agenda **C** blog

Do! **3** 🎯 Look and read. Choose the correct words and write them on the lines. There is one example.

tip **Exam**
Read all the definitions carefully before you start writing your answers.

a helmet   cycling

athletics

People often go to this in the summer when the weather is sunny. _____a beach_____

a diary

1 This is an indoor sport that people play with a small, plastic ball. _____

2 It's an outdoor activity for people who like plants and flowers. _____ sunglasses

3 You need a bike and a helmet to do this sport. _____

ice skating

4 You watch this and listen to a good singer or a band. _____

gardening

5 This is an outdoor sport. You need to be a good runner to do this. _____

6 This is a kind of book. Your write your ideas in it. _____

a concert 7 This is something hard that you wear on your head. _____ a ~~beach~~

table tennis   a CD player

Technology

Vocabulary

1 Complete the technology words.

| 1 | 2 | 3 | 4 | 5 | 6 |

e _arphones_   s_____   e-_____   s_____   p_____   l_____

2 Read and complete the messages.

> app   ~~devices~~   digital camera   password   screen   website

1 I have lots of electronic ____devices____ at home, but my favourite one is my _____. I want to be a photographer one day.

2 I bought a fashion magazine yesterday then I tried to visit their _____. It asked me for a _____, but I didn't have one.

3 There's a new _____ for smartphones. It shows you cartoon animals on the _____ and when you touch them, they make funny noises!

3 Read the *I'm learning* box. Then write three devices for each group.

I'm learning

Grouping words
Words are easier to learn and remember if you think about them as groups of similar things.

1 They have keyboards. _phone, computer, laptop_____
2 You can take photos with them. _____
3 You go online on them. _____
4 You can play videos on them. _____

4 Write three or more sentences about the devices that you have and what you use them for. Use the adverbs in the box.

> always   usually   often   sometimes   never

1 (2.4) **Listen and complete the sentences from the dialogue on Pupil's Book page 22. Then listen again and check.**

1 What's the ___matter___, Ting?

2 Did you _____ your password?

3 Did you _____ to start again?

4 You have to _____ it to her today.

5 I didn't send my Maths _____ last night.

6 I _____ write my homework again with this!

2 **Read the dialogue again and answer the questions. Write complete sentences.**

1 Who is going to be angry? *Miss Baker is going to be angry.*

2 What stopped working last night? _____

3 Whose computer did Ting use? _____

4 Why can't she print her work? _____

5 What does Bobby give to Ting? _____

6 What does she finally have to do? _____

3 (2.5) **Read and complete the dialogue with the correct expressions. Then listen and check.**

| Oh dear! | ~~Why not?~~ | You're joking! | Why not? |

Grandma: What are you doing, Susana?

Susana: I'm writing an email to my teacher.

Grandma: Oh! I didn't do that when I was a child.

Susana: Really? [1] _____Why not?_____

Grandma: We didn't have computers when I was at school.

Susana: [2] _____ You didn't use computers at school?

Grandma: No, we didn't. It's true.

Susana: [3] _____ That's terrible! I can't live without the internet.

Grandma: [4] _____ Do you have to be on your computer or your laptop all the time?

Susana: Yes, I do. I love my devices!

4 **Work in pairs. Write another dialogue using the expressions in Activity 3. Then act out the dialogue.**

could/couldn't, had to / didn't have to

1 (2.8) **Listen to Sarah and her grandma. Then circle the correct options.**

1 Sarah **couldn't** / **didn't have to** chat with her friends yesterday.

2 When Grandma was young, she **didn't have to** / **couldn't** write messages on a smartphone.

3 Grandma **could** / **had to** use the phone at home to speak to her friends.

4 Grandma and her friends **couldn't** / **didn't have to** meet up every day to chat.

5 Grandma **had to** / **couldn't** see her friends at cafés to have group conversations.

6 Grandma and her friends **had to** / **couldn't** write letters and take them to the post office.

2 **Look at the pictures from the past and complete the sentences. Use** *could/couldn't* **or** *had to / didn't have to*.

She ___had to___ walk to school because there wasn't a school bus.

He didn't have a TV, but he _____ listen to the radio.

She didn't have an e-reader, but she _____ read a book.

He _____ talk on a smartphone with his friends so they met at the park.

She played and ran outside so she _____ join a sports team.

He didn't have a computer, so he _____ write his homework in a notebook.

3 **Read and complete the sentences for you. Use** *could/couldn't* **or** *had to / didn't have to* **and the verb in brackets.**

1 When I was three years old, I ___didn't have to make___ (make) my bed.

2 I _____ (draw) very well when I was four years old.

3 When I was five, _____ (make) my lunch.

4 I _____ (do) a lot of homework when I was six.

5 When I was seven, I _____ (play) a musical instrument well.

6 I _____ (study) English when I was seven.

4 **Write four more sentences about your life in the past. Use** *could/couldn't* **and** *had to /didn't have to* **and the ideas in the box.**

> go to bed early   help my parents
> play sports   read well   ride a bike
> study a lot   tidy my room

_____

_____

_____

_____

5 **Compare your sentences from Activity 4 with your partner. Write their sentences in your notebook.**

>> Grammar reference, page 119

1 **After you read** **Read the poem on Pupil's Book page 24 again. Find and write words that rhyme.**

1 website   _right_
2 alone   _____
3 more   _____
4 down   _____

5 app   _____
6 internet   _____
7 brighter   _____
8 screen   _____

2 **Number the lines of the poem in order.**

a _____ It will take you safely back home.
b _____ Try the blue and white one.
c _____ Why not watch a video?
d _1_ It's better than my last phone.
e _____ You need some information.
f _____ It doesn't take so much time.
g _____ The phone can take them better.

3 **Read the *Work with words* box. Then write the adverbs.**

> **Work with words**
>
> **Adverbs ending in -ly**
> We can make adverbs by adding -*ly* to some adjectives:
> *quick* → *quick**ly***
> If the adjective ends in a consonant and -*y*, we change the -*y* to -*i*:
> *happy* → *happ**ily***

1 easy   _easily_
2 bad   _____
3 quiet   _____
4 noisy   _____
5 careful   _____
6 slow   _____

4 **Complete the sentences with the adverbs from Activity 3.**

1 I'm not very good at reading maps. I get lost very _____easily_____!
2 Tom doesn't talk a lot. He often sits _____ and reads.
3 My mother isn't a good artist. She draws quite _____.
4 Adam walks very _____. I always have to wait for him.
5 Please cross the street _____. Look both ways first!
6 The girls are playing _____. They're always so loud!

5 **Write five sentences about you, your friends and your family. Use the adverb form of the words in the box.**

bad   careful   clear   easy   nice   noisy   polite   quiet   safe   slow

Vocabulary and Grammar

1 **Read and circle the correct words.**

1 Don't (press) / go / upload a button if you don't know what it will do.

2 Let's **search** / **press** / **watch** a video tonight. How about Avatar?

3 We have to **download** / **type** / **click** a password to use the app.

4 Can you help me **upload** / **watch** / **type** a photo to my blog?

5 How many times do you **send** / **go** / **take** online every day?

6 I didn't **watch** / **turn** / **press** on the computer. Did you?

2 2.12 **Complete the sentences with two or three words. Then listen and check your guesses.**

1 I'm late. I have to *send a message* to my mum.

2 Please _____ the TV now. It's time for bed.

3 Mum says we can _____ from this website.

4 I want to _____ with my smartphone. Smile!

5 You _____ that icon to start the game.

6 Ben needs to _____ for facts for his Science project.

Comparative adverbs

3 **Write sentences about Tom and Lucy's schoolwork. Use comparative adverbs.**

		Tom	Lucy
1	listens carefully	✓	✗
2	studies hard	✗	✓
3	speaks clearly	✓	✗
4	works fast	✗	✓
5	learns easily	✓	✗
6	writes well	✗	✓

1 Tom *listens more carefully than Lucy.*

2 Lucy _____

3 Tom _____

4 Lucy _____

5 Tom _____

6 Lucy _____

4 **Write comparative sentences about you and your friends. Use the adverbs in the box and your own ideas. Then compare with your partner.**

> badly carefully clearly easily fast
> hard quietly slowly well

1 *I speak more clearly in English than my friend Emily.*

2 _____
_____

3 _____
_____

4 _____
_____

5 _____
_____

6 _____
_____

Grammar reference, page 119

1 **After you read** **Read the text on Pupil's Book page 26 again. Match.**

1 People are using technology
2 Children in Nigeria couldn't read
3 Many children have smartphones
4 Many South African children spend
5 The new Maths app gives children
6 When children use the Maths app,

☐ **a** and some of them have e-readers, too.
☐ **b** they can send messages to their class.
☐ **c** information and asks them questions.
[1] **d** to help children study and read better.
☐ **e** a lot of time on the internet.
☐ **f** very many books or stories.

2 **Answer the questions. Write complete sentences.**

1 Why are more Nigerian children reading e-books now?
   There is a big online library with lots of e-books.

2 Why couldn't Nigerian children read many books before?
   _____

3 What languages can they read stories in on their e-readers?
   _____

4 What school subject does the new South African app teach?
   _____

5 Who can help the South African children online?
   _____

6 Why are the children happy with the new app?
   _____

3 (2.14) **Listen and complete the notes.**

Programme:	OLPC, which means One ¹ _Laptop_ Per ² _____ .
Objective:	Making ³_____ and ⁴_____ laptops for children in developing countries.
Reason:	Children take the laptops ⁵_____ to share them with their ⁶_____ .
Use:	The laptops are connected together at ⁷_____ and children can use the ⁸_____ .

4 📶 **Work in groups. Think about laptops and find answers to the questions. Write about what you found out. Then share your information with the class.**

1 What do you use to type on a laptop?
2 What part of the laptop shows images?
3 Where does the electricity come from?
4 Where does the laptop keep information?
5 How do you connect a laptop to a printer?
6 What other devices are used with a laptop?

English in action
Asking for help

1 (2.17) **Read and complete the dialogue. Then listen and check.**

at the screen   my Science project   search the internet   that button
this evening   tidy the garage   want to do   ~~your laptop~~

Dan: Please can I use ¹___*your laptop*___, Mum?

Mum: Of course. What do you ²_____?

Dan: ³_____. I want to look at a science website. Can you show me how to turn it on?

Mum: That's easy. Press ⁴_____ there.

Dan: OK. What next?

Mum: Look ⁵_____. Click on that icon over there.

Dan: Thanks. Do you have time to help me with ⁶_____?

Mum: Sorry, not now. I have to ⁷_____.

Dan: Alright. Could you help me ⁸_____, please?

Mum: Of course.

2 **Read the questions and number the pictures. Then match the questions and answers.**

1 Do you have time to tidy the kitchen? [c]

2 Could you go to the supermarket, please? [ ]

3 Can I use your laptop to write an email? [ ]

4 Do you have time to help me study? [ ]

5 Can you show me how to start this app? [ ]

6 Please can I use your printer to print my homework? [ ]

a That's easy. Touch that icon there.

b Of course. What do I need to buy?

c Not right now. I'm going cycling.

d Of course. Do you have a test?

e Of course. Do you want to print it now?

f Sorry, not now. I'm using it at the moment.

 [ ]
 [ ]
 [ ]

 [ ]
 [ ]
 [1]

Pronunciation

3 💬 (2.18) **Circle the word *to* in the questions in Activity 2. Then listen and repeat. Notice the short sound. Then practise with your partner.**

Reading

Words in context

1 Read and complete the sentences.

~~solve~~   challenge   program   score   give   play

1 When you need to _____*solve*_____ a problem, it often helps to ask a friend.
2 That game is too easy. _____ yourself with something difficult!
3 I want to learn how to _____ a computer, so I can design games.
4 In that game, players _____ points by collecting secret messages.
5 If you want to _____ online, you need a fast internet connection.
6 You can _____ tips to your friends so you can all play the game better.

2 Read the text on Pupil's Book page 28 again. Who gives these facts about TopCity? Write *GameFan* or *MrCool001*.

1 Two or more people can play together.   _____*MrCool001*_____
2 The problems get more difficult as you play.   _____
3 You have to visit all the buildings in the city.   _____
4 The game can't be used with all phones.   _____
5 Players write instructions to move around.   _____
6 The game gives you tips to play better.   _____

3 Answer the questions. Write complete sentences.

1 What do TopCity players search for during the game?
   They search for treasure.

2 What does MrCool001 think about the price of the game?

3 What device does GameFan use to play the game?

4 What does MrCool001 enjoy the most about the game?

5 What does GameFan have to do before he can start playing?

6 How did MrCool001 learn to play the game better?

4 Work in groups. Discuss the survey questions and make notes. Then share your ideas with the class.

1 What computer programmes do you use the most?
2 What are your favourite computer games? Why?
3 What apps do you have on your smartphone?
4 How long are you usually online every day?

Literacy: Reviews

Writing

1 **Read CameraKid's notes. Then complete the review.**

tip **Writing**
When you plan, make notes. You don't need to write sentences!

☆☆☆☆☆ – **Easy and fun!**

really like PhotoForum,

keen on photography; lots of my

friends use same app

Good: can join lots of groups, write

comments; quite a good app, very

simple, easy to use; basic tools for

editing your photos; app is cheap –

only 2 euros

Bad: only see 4 photos on the screen

at one time, can't send any photos in

private messages

☆☆☆☆☆ – **Easy and fun!**

by CameraKid

I use PhotoForum because I'm [1] _____ *keen* _____ on photography.
A lot of my friends use this [2] _____, too.

Good points:

1 There are lots of [3] _____ to join. Then you write comments about people's photos.

2 It's quite a good app because it's [4] _____ and it isn't hard to use.

3 The app has [5] _____ tools to edit photos quickly and easily. Some are fun too!

4 Photo-Forum is cheap, too. It only costs [6] _____, which isn't expensive.

Bad points:

1 You can only see [7] _____ photos at once. Other apps do this better, with more photos on the screen.

2 You can't send photos in private [8] _____ to friends. That's a problem for me!

2 **Make some notes to plan a review about an app or game you use.**

Give the app or game a rating, e.g. 3 star. Give your review a title.

Write an introduction. Explain why you use the app or game.

List three or four good points about it.

List two or three bad points about it.

3 **Now write your review.**

4 **Check your work. Tick (✓) the steps when you have done them.**

Have I included a short introduction? ☐

Have I included good and bad points? ☐

Have I used adjectives correctly? ☐

Have I used adverbs correctly? ☐

1 Read the sentences. What do they describe?

1 It's a light computer that you can carry around. _____a laptop_____
2 You use this to take photos. You can't go online on it. _____
3 You use this so other people can't hear your loud music. _____
4 It's a special device for reading electronic books. _____
5 You must remember this and keep it a secret. _____
6 It's a programme you can download to a phone. _____

2 Unscramble the technology phrases.

1 og lenoin _____go online_____
2 rtnu no eth vt _____
3 serps a tnbotu _____
4 cwhat a oveid _____
5 dnse a smsegae _____
6 cerhas het trenetni _____
7 ilckc no na nico _____
8 keat a filese _____

3 Read and complete the sentences. Use the correct form of the verbs in the box.

1 Sam _____had to help_____ his parents when he was little. He tidied up the house.
2 When I was five, I _____ a bike. I learned when I was six.
3 My sister is very musical. She _____ the piano when she was seven!
4 We _____ our stories to the class. We gave them to the teacher.
5 Emma _____ home early today. She wasn't feeling very well.
6 They _____ the app because they didn't know the password.

go | help | play | not/open | not/read | not/ride

4 Compare yourself to other people. Use the comparative form of the adverbs.

1 write / well _____I write better than my brother._____
2 read / fast _____
3 speak / clearly _____
4 sing / badly _____
5 study / hard _____
6 listen / carefully _____

Self-evaluation

5 Answer the questions about your work in Unit 2.

1 How was your work in this unit? Choose. ☐ OK ☐ Good ☐ Excellent
2 Which lesson was your favourite? _____
3 Which parts of the unit were difficult for you? _____
4 What new things can you talk about now? _____
5 How can you work and learn better in the next unit? _____

Get ready for...

Think! **1** Read the task carefully. Make sure you know what you have to do.

Try! **2** What can you see in the picture in Activity 3? Tick (✓).

✓ a guitar	☐ a laptop	☐ a garden	☐ a camera
☐ a puzzle	☐ a backpack	☐ a smartphone	☐ a printer
☐ a TV screen	☐ a volleyball	☐ a window	☐ earphones

Do! **3** 🎯 🎧 2.21 Listen and colour and write.

tip Exam

Listen very carefully the first time before you colour or write. Listen the second time to check your answers.

A2 Flyers Reading and Writing Part 2

Think! **1** Read the task carefully. Make sure you know what you have to do.

Try! **2** Match the questions to the correct answers. Draw lines.

1 Does your mum have a tablet?

2 Have you finished your project?

3 When did Sarah upload the photo?

4 Which smartphone do you want to buy?

5 Why didn't you watch that video?

A No, I couldn't do it.

B Last night, I think.

C I had to tidy my room.

D Yes. She loves it.

E This one. It's cheaper.

Do! **3** 🎯 Lorena is asking Rodrigo some questions. What does Rodrigo say? Read the conversation and choose the best answer. Write a letter (A–H) for each answer. You do not need to use all the letters. There is one example.

tip Exam

Once all of the gaps are completed, read through all your responses again to make sure they make sense.

Example
Lorena: Did you go shopping for a laptop yesterday?
Rodrigo: _F_

1 Lorena: Do you know what laptop you want to buy?
Rodrigo: ___

2 Lorena: How much money do you want to spend?
Rodrigo: ___

3 Lorena: Have you looked at the Computerland website?
Rodrigo: ___

4 Lorena: Would you like me to go shopping with you today?
Rodrigo: ___

5 Lorena: What time would you like to go shopping?
Rodrigo: ___

A I think two o'clock would be good.

B Yes, but their laptops are expensive.

C I think so, but it's hard to decide!

D There was an e-reader that I liked.

E Sure! That would be great!

F No, I didn't. I had to study.

G I couldn't see anyone there.

H Not a lot. I don't need the best one.

3 Places

Vocabulary

1 **Read the clues and complete the crossword.**

1 a place you go to when you are sick
2 a beautiful home for a king or queen
3 a tall building or part of a building
4 a modern building that is extremely tall
5 a building where people make things
6 a place where large boats can stop
7 a place where you can watch football
8 a very safe place to live in the past

(crossword: 1 across = H O S P I T A L)

2 **Complete the places in the city.**

~~building~~   building   centre   shop   office   pool   station   centre

1 office _____building_____
2 toy _____
3 sports _____
4 swimming _____
5 shopping _____
6 train _____
7 apartment _____
8 post _____

3 💡 **Read the *I'm learning* box. Then write the definitions.**

I'm learning

Describing places
You can describe places by saying what you do there.

A stadium is a place where you can watch football.

1 hospital *A hospital is a place where you can see a doctor.*
2 sports centre _____
3 office building _____
4 shopping centre _____
5 bookshop _____
6 swimming pool _____

4 💡 **Write about three or more places near your home. What can you do there? Use words from this lesson and your own ideas.**

1 (3.4) **Complete the sentences from the dialogue on Pupil's Book page 34. Who said them? Write. Then listen and check.**

behind   hospital   place   remember   ~~stadium~~   online

1 ___Lara___   Oh, dear! Where's the ___stadium___ ?

2 _____   I didn't like it in _____.

3 _____   The stadium is right _____ us!

4 _____   What's this big _____?

5 _____   The Wi-Fi wasn't very good and I couldn't go _____.

6 _____   Oh, yes. I _____.

2 **Read the dialogue again and circle _T_ (true) or _F_ (false). Explain your answers.**

1 Lara learned to swim at the sports centre.   **T /(F)**

   Ting learned to swim at the sports centre.

2 The stadium is near the hospital where Ting was in April.   **T / F**

_____

3 The girls went to a factory where people make chocolate.   **T / F**

_____

4 Ting was the only person who felt sick after visiting the factory.   **T / F**

_____

5 The doctors that Ting met at the hospital were friendly.   **T / F**

_____

6 The girls didn't see the stadium on the street map.   **T / F**

_____

3 (3.5) **Complete the dialogues with the correct expressions. Then listen and check.**

(Right) x 2   (No way!) x 2   (Hey, look!) x 2

1 A: I've never seen a football match.

   B: _No way!_ That can't be true. It's a great game!

2 A: _____ Is that Lisa?

   B: Yes, it is. Let's go and talk to her.

3 A: Tom's meeting us at the café at four o'clock.

   B: _____ Let's go!

4 A: Where's the bus? It's always late.

   B: _____ There it is now.

5 A: Our Science project is due next week.

   B: _____ We need to decide what to do it on.

6 A: I don't have a mobile phone.

   B: _____ Why not?

4 **Work in pairs. Write another dialogue for each expression. Then act out the dialogues.**

Grammar

Relative pronouns

1 (3.8) **Listen to the conversation and tick (✓) the correct pictures.**

1 It's the country that Tom is going to go to.

 a Italy

 b France ✓

2 It's a person who is travelling with Tom.

 a

 b

3 It's the month when Tom wants to travel.

 a

 b

4 It's the place where they're going to stay.

 a

 b

5 It's a famous place which Tom's wants to visit.

 a

 b

2 **Circle the correct relative pronouns.**

1 A baker is a person **who** / **which** / **where** bakes bread and pastries.

2 The football match **when** / **that** / **where** we saw last week was great!

3 Home is the place **that** / **who** / **where** I feel the most relaxed.

4 Summer is the time **which** / **when** / **who** most people have holidays.

5 The people **which** / **when** / **who** help me the most are my family.

6 This is the e-book **who** / **which** / **when** I bought last week.

3 **Complete the sentences. Use relative pronouns.**

are always there for you   people give you presents
sells fruit and vegetables   trees drop their leaves
you should use carefully   you can learn about history

1 Your birthday is the day *when people give you presents*.

2 A museum is a place _____.

3 Friends are people _____.

4 A smartphone is a device _____.

5 Autumn is the season _____.

6 A greengrocer is someone _____.

4 **Write sentences with relative pronouns. Use the words below and your own ideas.**

1 a person / makes me laugh

2 a place / I like to spend time

3 the time of year / I feel best

4 a sport / I often play or watch

5 a person / I'd love to meet

6 a device / I want to buy

1 *My friend Oli is a person who makes me laugh.*

2 _____

3 _____

4 _____

5 _____

6 _____

5 💬 **Compare your sentences from Activity 4 with your partner. Do you have similar answers? Write their sentences in your notebook.**

》》 Grammar reference, page 120

1 **After you read** **Read the narrative story on Pupil's Book page 36 again. Number the events in order.**

- [ ] **a** Carrie and Eddie followed the guide up the stairs.
- [ ] **b** A girl in a green dress gave Eddie a paintbrush.
- [ ] **c** Eddie and Carrie ran to the steps at the front of Bingley Palace.
- [ ] **d** The guide told the visitors about Lady Charlotte.
- [ ] **e** Eddie woke up and found something in his pocket.
- [ ] **f** Eddie noticed something strange about the painting.
- [1] **g** Carrie called to Eddie and told him that they were late.
- [ ] **h** Eddie fell into a secret room behind the bookcase.

2 **Answer the questions. Write complete sentences.**

1 Where was Eddie when Carrie told him they were late?

He was under a tree in front of the palace.

2 What was the first room that the visitors saw in the palace?

_____

3 Where was the picture of the woman in the green dress?

_____

4 What did Eddie notice about the windows in the picture?

_____

5 Why did everything go black after the bookcase moved?

_____

6 Where do you think the paintbrush came from?

_____

3 **Read the *Work with words* box. Then look and write the compound nouns.**

Work with words

Compound nouns
Some nouns are compound nouns which are made with two words.

sketch + book = sketchbook
book + case = bookcase

1
~~arm~~ bath book ~~chair~~ dish room shop washer

2
brush ear fighter fire home paint phones work

3
ball board fall market skate super volley water

1 *armchair* _____
2 _____
3 _____

4 💡 **Write definitions for five words from Activity 3. Use relative pronouns.**

1 (3.12) **Listen and complete the sentences with one, two or three words.**

1 We live on the ___second floor___ of the apartment building, so I usually take the lift.

2 The sports hall is at the end of that _____ over there.

3 My grandma's favourite chair is the blue one _____ of the sitting room.

4 If there's a fire in the building, follow the signs to the emergency _____.

5 We walked up the _____ of the building and through the main door.

6 There's a café _____ of that building. It has a nice view.

2 **Look at the pictures. Complete the sentences.**

1 There's a picture on the ___wall___.

2 The armchair is in the _____.

3 There's a lamp on the _____.

4 The dog is on the _____.

5 This is the _____ to the underground.

6 Two people are on the _____.

7 There's a man on the _____.

8 A woman is next to the _____.

Past continuous

3 **Complete the sentences with the Past continuous of the verbs in the box.**

> not/do sit not/work visit talk
> not/watch wait

1 Samuel ___was sitting___ outside on the steps when it started to rain.

2 When I got home from school, my dad _____ TV.

3 You _____ to Emily when we saw you at the café today.

4 When you called Tom and Kate, they _____ their homework.

5 I _____ a castle when I noticed a strange painting on the wall.

6 When the swimming pool opened, we _____ in the queue.

7 The lift _____ when I tried to use it, so I walked up the stairs.

4 💡 **Complete the sentences with information that is true for you. Use the Past continuous.**

1 When I woke up yesterday, my ___brother___ ___was having a shower.___

2 When I arrived at school, my friends _____.

3 When I entered the classroom, our teacher _____.

4 When I got home after school, my _____.

5 When my parents called me for dinner, I _____.

6 When my friend texted me, I _____.

>> Grammar reference, page 120

1 **After you read** **Read the sentences. Write _T_ (true), _F_ (false) or _DS_ (doesn't say). Explain your answers.**

1 Pompeii was a small town when the volcano covered it.

[_F_] _It was a city when the volcano covered it._

2 Some archaeologists started digging under people's houses.

[ ] _____

3 Pompeii had a theatre where people could watch plays.

[ ] _____

4 A British man found some small castles in Mohenjo Daro.

[ ] _____

5 The buildings tell us what life was like in Mohenjo Daro.

[ ] _____

6 In Mohenjo Daro, people didn't have baths in their homes.

[ ] _____

2 **Answer the questions. Write complete sentences.**

1 Why should we study ancient cities and buildings? _We should study them because they can tell us about the past._

2 How long ago did the volcano cover Pompeii with ash? _____

3 What did the ancient Romans do to some walls in Pompeii? _____

4 Who found and uncovered the city of Mohenjo Daro? _____

5 How do we know that there were toilets in Mohenjo Daro? _____

3 (3.14) **Listen and complete the notes.**

• **Ancient city:**	[1] _Chichen Itza_
• **Location:**	It's in the Yucatan region of [2] _____. It's located [3] _____ Mérida and Cancún.
• **History:**	The city is more than [4] _____ years old. It was an important Mayan city, but then people started to leave. After everyone left, the [5] _____ covered the city.
• **Famous places:**	The Castillo pyramid is about [6] _____ metres high. There's a [7] _____ where the Mayans played games.
• **Amazing fact:**	More than two million tourists visit Chichen Itza.

4 📶 **Work in groups. Choose the ancient city of Angkor or Thebes and find answers to the questions. Write about your ancient city. Then make a factfile about it.**

1 Where is it located?
2 How old is the city?
3 Why was it important?

4 Why did people leave the city?
5 What are the most famous places there?

English in action
Giving directions in a building

1 (3.17) **Complete the dialogue. Then listen and check.**

a On the second floor? Is there an escalator? **d** And what about the toilets? Where are they, please?
b Yes, I am. I'm a big fan of Pablo Picasso. **e** Yes, it is. I'm learning about art at school.
c ~~Thank you. Good morning to you too.~~ **f** Can you tell me where the modern art room is?

Man: Good morning. Welcome to the art gallery.

Girl: ¹ *c. Thank you. Good morning to you too.* _____

Man: Is this your first visit to the art gallery?

Girl: ² _____

Man: Really! Are you enjoying it?

Girl: ³ _____

Man: Oh, Picasso's paintings are very interesting.

Girl: ⁴ _____

Man: Yes, of course. It's upstairs on the second floor.

Girl: ⁵ _____

Man: No, there isn't, but there is a lift. Go down that corridor.

Girl: ⁶ _____

Man: They're on the ground floor, next to the café.

2 **Circle the correct words.**

1 You can go up in the (**lift**) / **doors** to the history room. Then go **around** / **along** the corner.

2 Is the café the first **floor** / **door** on the right or the second on the **left** / **straight**?

3 You go **through** / **up** those two doors and then **around** / **along** the corridor.

4 The toilets are **down** / **straight** on and **around** / **left** the corner.

5 There wasn't **an escalator** / **a corridor** so I took the **stairs** / **downstairs** to the first floor.

3 **Choose one of the following places and write another dialogue. Use the model in Activity 1 to help you. Then act it out with your partner.**

| an art gallery a castle a library |
| a museum a palace |

Pronunciation

4 (3.18) 💬 **Listen and match. Then listen and repeat. Notice the short sounds of *was* and *were*. Then practise with your partner.**

1 I	were drawing	Roman art.
2 They	was going	for the café.
3 Kate	were visiting	a mystery novel.
4 We	was reading	up the stairs.
5 You	was looking	an old castle.
6 Tom	were studying	a picture of me.

Literacy: short stories

Reading

1 **Read and complete the sentences. Then match to the pictures.**

> sketched   zoomed   yelled   remembered
> whispered   smiled

1 The artist _____sketched_____ a castle in his notebook.
2 Jessie _____ and felt happy about her dream.
3 We _____ because we were in the library.
4 You _____ my birthday. You never forget!
5 The motorbike _____ quickly down the street.
6 Kelly _____ at me when I broke her new tablet.

2 **Read the story on Pupil's Book page 40 again. Match.**

1 Jessie wanted to write a story [e]   a she was lying in her bed.
2 She felt quite happy when [ ]   b and it flew out of the window.
3 Jessie heard a noise when [ ]   c she finished her drawing of the bird.
4 She was very surprised when [ ]   d over the people in the harbour.
5 Jessie jumped onto the bird [ ]   e but she didn't have any ideas.
6 She yelled when they flew [ ]   f the bird started talking to her.

3 **Answer the questions. Write complete sentences.**

1 Why was Jessie surprised when she saw the bird?

   Because it was the bird from her drawing.

2 What did Jessie feel scared about at first?

   _____

3 What buildings did Jessie see when she was flying?

   _____

4 Why did Jessie feel sad when she woke up?

   _____

5 Why did Jessie smile before she started to write?

   _____

6 What do you think she saw at the end of the story?

   _____

4 **Work in groups to make the story longer. Imagine what happens to Jessie after she sees the harbour and before she goes home. Use the ideas below. Then share your ideas with the class.**

- After Jessie sees the harbour …
- Then the bird …
- Jessie sees …
- Then they fly to …
- Jessie feels …

Writing

tip Writing

1 **Read what the people said. Then complete the sentences.**

> Do you want to fly?   Don't press that button!   I don't like football.
> That room is closed.   Don't tell anyone.   You're too slow!

tip Writing
Show the words
that people say
like this:
'Ouch!' he shouted.
'My foot hurts!'
'A concert just for
me!' Daniel said,
with a big smile on
his face.

1 '_____*I don't like football*_____', Kevin said.
'I prefer basketball.'

2 '_____', I whispered quietly.
'It's a secret!'

3 The bird asked me, '_____'
and I said, 'Yes, please!'

4 '_____', the boys yelled,
so I started walking faster.

5 The guide said, '_____',
so we couldn't go in.

6 Emma shouted, '_____'
and everything went black.

2 **Plan a short story.**

| Setting: Where and when does the story take place? |
| Characters: Who are the characters in the story? They can be people, animals or something else. |
| Beginning: How does your story begin? |
| Middle: What happens in the middle? |
| End: How does your story end? |

3 **Now write your short story.**

4 **Check your work. Tick (✓) the steps when you have done them.**

Have I included all the parts of
the story? ☐

Have I written what the characters
said correctly? ☐

Have I used the past tenses correctly? ☐

Have I included some relative pronouns? ☐

1 Write the names of the places.

1 _apartment building_
2 _____
3 _____
4 _____
5 _____
6 _____
7 _____
8 _____

2 Order the letters to complete the sentences.

1 I had an accident. I fell down the _steps_ (tessp) at school.

2 Go along the _____ (irordcro) and then turn right.

3 We need to paint the _____ (nicgeli) in that room.

4 Buy a ticket at the _____ (arnenetc) to the museum.

5 This _____ (asltrecoa) goes up, but I want to go down.

6 I left my bag in the _____ (rorcen) of the room and now it isn't there!

3 Complete the definitions. Use relative pronouns.

1 A librarian is a person _who works at a library._

2 A castle is a place _____

3 Summer is a time _____

4 A lift is something _____

5 A doctor is a person _____

6 A paintbrush is an object _____

4 Write Past continuous sentences.

1 My dad / not / cook / phone / ring — _My dad wasn't cooking when the phone rang_

2 I / play football / it / start / snow — _____

3 My mum / sing / bus / arrive — _____

4 It / not / rain / we / walk / school — _____

5 They / buy / laptop / shop assistant / yell — _____

Self-evaluation

5 Answer the questions about your work in Unit 3.

1 How was your work in this unit? Choose. ☐ OK ☐ Good ☐ Excellent

2 Which lesson was your favourite? _____

3 Which parts of the unit were difficult for you? _____

4 What new things can you talk about now? _____

5 How can you work and learn better in the next unit? _____

Get ready for...

 1 Read the task carefully. Make sure you know what you have to do.

 2 🎧 3.20 **Listen and choose the correct answers.**

1 What time is the football match?   **A** 5.00   **B** 5.15   **C** 5.30

2 What day is the concert?   **A** Tuesday   **B** Wednesday   **C** Thursday

3 What is the girl's name?   **A** Jonson   **B** Jensen   **C** Johnson

Do! **3** 🎯 🎧 3.21 **Listen. For each question, choose the correct answer.**

tip Exam

Look at the picture and the text before you listen. They can give you helpful information.

The Ancient History Club

The club meets: at ___4.30 pm___ on Wednesdays

1 The children in the club often visit: _____

2 The club has parties when children wear: _____

3 The children in the club have to buy: _____

4 The President of the club is: Mrs _____

5 Club members must be: _____ years old

A2 Flyers Reading and Writing Part 3

Think! **1** Read the task carefully. Make sure you know what you have to do.

Try! **2** Choose the correct words to complete the sentences.

1 When I was in New York, I saw a baseball **show** / (**game**) / **play** at the stadium.
2 Tourists can buy nice postcards at the castle's gift **office** / **museum** / **shop**.
3 I'd like to visit a big **city** / **harbour** / **factory** where we can go shopping for clothes.
4 You can't use the **stair** / **lift** / **entrance** at the moment. There isn't any electricity.
5 Excuse me. I'm looking for the **floor** / **corner** / **exit**. Do you know where it is?
6 Please don't **yell** / **whisper** / **smile** in the library. You must be very quiet!

Do! **3** Read the story. Write the correct word from the box next to numbers 1–5. There is one example.

tip Exam
Read the whole text and all the words in the box before you start writing.

ceiling   clouds   leave   lights   office   roof   stairs   stay   tower   weather

Last summer, I went to London to visit my cousin. One day, my cousin took me to a tall ____office____ building in the centre of the city. There was nice café on the **(1)**_____ where we could look out and see the whole city and the river. While we were there the **(2)**_____ changed and it started raining a lot. Suddenly, all the **(3)**_____ went out. There wasn't any electricity! The lift wasn't working and there were too many **(4)**_____ to walk down, so we waited. It was boring, but a boy started playing the guitar, and then a girl started singing! They were excellent! When the lights finally came back on, everyone wanted to **(5)**_____ and hear more music!

(6) Now choose the best title for the story. Tick (✓) one box.

The tall tower ☐   London weather ☐   Singing on the roof ☐

Language booster 1

1 **Look and match.**

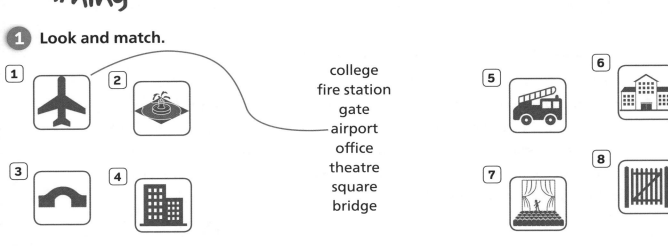

college
fire station
gate
airport
office
theatre
square
bridge

2 **Read and complete the sentences.**

gate   college   ~~bridge~~   fire station   square   airport   office   theatre

1 You can't go across the river here. There isn't a _____*bridge*_____!

2 My sister is studying science at the _____ .

3 A lot of planes fly over my house because we live near the _____ .

4 My mum works in a big _____ . She helps people with computer problems.

5 I want to be an actor and work in a _____ !

6 There's a statue in the middle of the _____ in our town.

7 Our house number is 57. You can see the number on the _____ .

8 My dad is a firefighter. He works at the _____ .

3 **Read and draw the directions.**

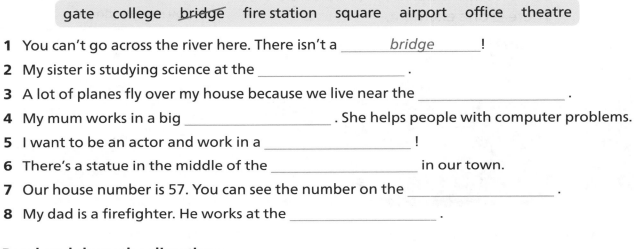

across   along   over   past   around   through

4 **Read and circle the directions.**

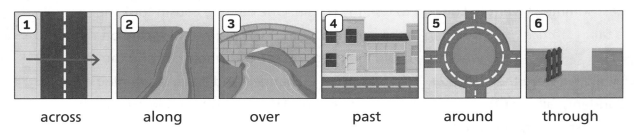

When I leave the swimming pool, what should I do?

Go **along / through** the river and **straight on / over** the bridge. Go **past / straight on**. Then go **across / around** the road and **along / past** the theatre. My house is next to the park. You go **over / through** a big gate. See you soon!

5 (LB1.3) **Listen and look at the map. Start at A and follow the routes. Write _B_, _C_, _D_ or _E_ below.**

1 _____   2 _____   3 _____   4 _____

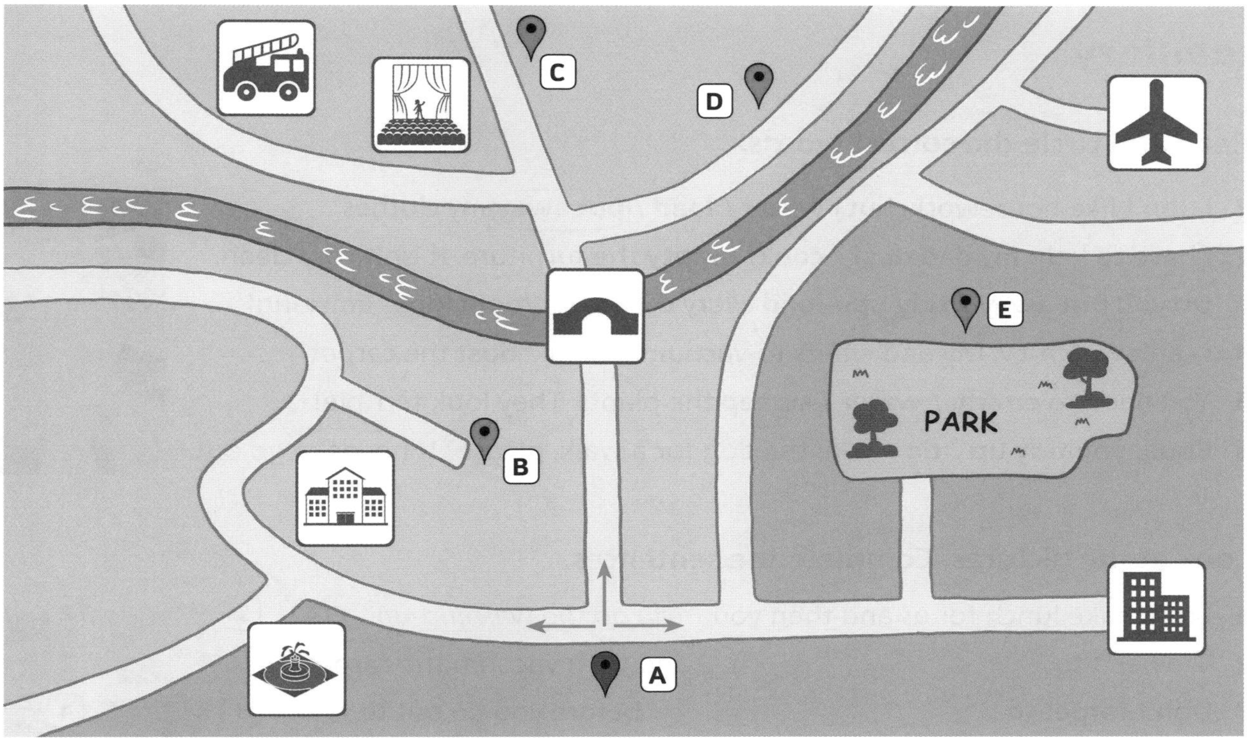

6 **Look at the map in Activity 5 and complete the directions. Start at A.**

1 Can you tell me the way to the office, please?

Of course! Turn ___right___ and go _____ .

2 Can you tell me the way to the square, please?

Turn _____, and then turn _____ again. The square is on your left.

3 Can you tell me the way to the airport, please?

Yes, I can. Turn _____ and then take the first _____ . Go _____ the river, and take the second _____ .

7 **Write directions to the fire station. Start at A.**

_____

_____

_____

Happy homes

Vocabulary

1 **Read and circle the correct words.**

1 I don't like housework, but I **water** / **load** / (**put away**) my clothes.

2 I have to help my dad **dust** / **cook** / **empty** the furniture. It isn't very clean.

3 Do you **put away** / **tidy up** / **load** every day? Your room looks amazing!

4 I can't watch TV. My dad wants to **vacuum** / **clear** / **dust** the carpet.

5 You need to **empty** / **water** / **sweep** the plants. They look terrible!

6 Could you **tidy up** / **do** / **take** the dog for a walk, please? It needs to go out.

2 **Look at the pictures. Complete the sentences.**

1 I can make lunch for us and then you _can do the washing-up_ , OK?

2 We need to _____ and then vacuum the carpet.

3 Don't forget to _____ before you go out today.

4 I never _____ because my parents always do that.

5 It's your turn to _____. I did it yesterday.

6 Please _____ before you do your homework.

3 Read the *I'm learning* box. Then read and complete the sentences for you. Use phrases from this lesson and your own ideas.

> **I'm learning**
>
> **Describing your life**
> New language is easier to remember when you use it to describe your life and habits.
>
> *I always tidy up.*
> *I sometimes clear the table.*
> *I never dust the furniture.*

1 I usually _tidy up once a week_ . I also _wash the car for_ _my parents_ .

2 I sometimes _____, but I never _____.

3 I often _____ and I always _____.

4 I _____. I also _____.

5 I never _____ and I don't _____.

4 Write three or more sentences about you and your family. What jobs at home does each person do? Use the adverbs in the box.

> always   usually   often   sometimes   never

1 (4.4) **Complete the sentences from the dialogue on Pupil's Book page 50. Who says them? Write. Then listen and check.**

bins cake floor ~~mess~~ now tidy

1 _Arlo_ Cool! But look at the __mess__ over here!
2 _____ And we haven't swept the _____ yet.
3 _____ Well, we've already made the _____!
4 _____ What a mess! Hurry up, we have to _____ up.
5 _____ So she's coming _____? Quick! Hide!
6 _____ Has anyone emptied the _____ yet?

2 **Read the dialogue again and circle T (true) or F (false). Explain your answers.**

1 Lara's cake isn't ready when she arrives. T / **F**
   Bobby has already made the cake.

2 Bobby has already done the washing-up. T / F
   _____

3 The floor isn't dirty because Arlo cleaned it. T / F
   _____

4 Ting tells the boys that the bins are empty. T / F
   _____

5 Arlo receives a message that says 'OMW'. T / F
   _____

6 Lara is surprised, but it isn't her birthday. T / F
   _____

3 (4.5) **Complete the dialogues with the correct expressions. Then listen and check.**

(Surprise!) x 2   (Hang on!) x 2   (What a mess!) x 2

1 **A:** Where did these flowers come from?
   B: _____Surprise!_____ They're for you!

2 **A:** Oh, no! I dropped the milk!
   B: _____ Let's clean it up.

3 **A:** These papers should go in the bin.
   B: _____ That's my homework!

4 **A:** Look at this room! _____
   B: I know. I have to tidy it up.

5 **A:** I can't wait for you. I'm leaving now.
   B: _____ I only need a minute.

6 **A:** I hate my phone. It's so old.
   B: _____ Here's a new one!

4 **Work in pairs. Write another dialogue for each expression. Then act out the dialogues.**

Present perfect with *already*, *just* and *yet*

1 🎧 **4.8** **Listen and look at the picture. Circle the six mistakes.**

2 <u>Underline</u> **the mistakes and write the correct sentences.**

1 Amy hasn't cleared <u>yet</u> the table after lunch.
   Amy hasn't cleared the table for lunch yet.

2 Have already you swept the kitchen floor?
   _____

3 Mum and I have just load the dishwasher.
   _____

4 Thomas has dusted the furniture just.
   _____

5 Carlotta just has emptied the bins.
   _____

6 We've already water all of the plants.
   _____

3 **Read the text. Then write sentences with the Present perfect and *already*, *just* or *yet*.**

> It's 6.00 pm on Saturday. Kevin arrived home five minutes ago. He has to tidy his room now. Mum's in the living room. She vacuumed the carpet earlier. Then she had a coffee. Now she wants to water the plants. Dad's in the kitchen. He finished the washing-up two minutes ago. He doesn't need to cook the dinner. He did that an hour ago.

1 Kevin / arrive / home
   Kevin has just arrived home.

2 He / tidy / his room
   _____

3 Mum / vacuum / the carpet
   _____

4 She / water / the plants
   _____

5 Dad / do / the washing-up
   _____

4 **Write questions about today. Use the Present perfect and *yet*.**

1 have / breakfast
   Have you had breakfast yet?

2 tidy / your room
   _____

3 a teacher / speak to you
   _____

4 use / your smartphone
   _____

5 send / a message
   _____

5 💬 **Work with your partner. Ask them your questions from Activity 4 and write their answers in your notebook.**

》》 Grammar reference, page 121

 **Book Club**

1 **After you read** Read the play on Pupil's Book page 52 again. Who says these lines? Write.

1 _____Lulu_____ We need knives, forks and spoons.

2 _____ Come for lunch! I've already baked a cake.

3 _____ Anansi jumped in the river to wash his legs.

4 _____ Hi Anansi, have you had lunch yet?

5 _____ It smells like chocolate cake.

6 _____ I've already chopped the vegetables.

2 Read the sentences and circle *T* (true) or *F* (false). Explain your answers.

1 Ronny doesn't want any help from Anansi. **T / (F)** _Ronny says Anansi can help._

2 Kiki says she hasn't swept the floor yet. **T / F** _____

3 Henry has already boiled the vegetables. **T / F** _____

4 Lulu put salt on the food before cooking it. **T / F** _____

5 Anansi waited in the park before lunch. **T / F** _____

6 Anansi's legs became much shorter. **T / F** _____

3 Read the *Work with words* box. Then look and make collocations.

> **Work with words**
>
> **Collocations: verb + noun**
> Collocations are phrases with two or more parts.
> Some have a verb and a noun.
>
> *sweep + the floor*
> *empty + the bin*
> *do + the washing-up*

1 I've already baked _____a cake_____ for the party.

2 You have to feed _____ now. It's hungry.

3 Can you lay _____ for dinner, please?

4 Let's make _____ for lunch.

5 I read _____ to my sister every night.

6 Have you posted _____ I gave you yet?

4 Write five sentences about you, your friends and your family. Use the collocations in the box or any other collocations you know.

> visit a castle   go scooting   load the dishwasher   play volleyball
> press a button   go online   do puzzles   write a diary

1 **Label the picture. Then complete the sentences.**

1 I'd like some _____salt_____ on my chips, please.

2 Do you want some _____ on your food?

3 I can use _____ to eat noodles. What about you?

4 This _____ doesn't cut very well.

5 You need a _____ to eat your soup.

6 I can't eat my carrots. I don't have a _____.

2 **(4.12) Listen to the recipe and number the verbs in order. Then complete the dialogue.**

☐ add   ☐ boil   ☐ cut

☐ bake   [1] chop   ☐ mix

Mum: Can you help me cook the dinner, Paul?

Paul: Sure. What can I do?

Mum: Well, you can ¹_____chop_____ some vegetables. Then we have to ²_____ them for five minutes.

Paul: And what are you doing?

Mum: I'm preparing some chicken. First I ³_____ it into pieces. Then I ⁴_____ it with the vegetables.

Paul: OK. And then what?

Mum: We have to ⁵_____ some salt and pepper. Then we ⁶_____ it in the oven.

Paul: That sounds good!

Sense verbs: *look, smell, taste, sound, feel*

3 **Complete the sentences with the correct form of the verbs. Match.**

| feel   look   smell   sound   taste |

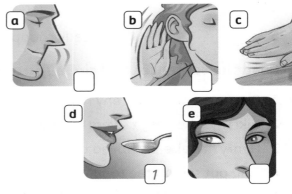

1 How much salt did you add to the soup? It _____tastes_____ really salty!

2 Who's singing that song? It _____ like Elvis Presley.

3 Your shoes _____ so pretty. I love the colour.

4 Mmm. Those cupcakes _____ delicious! I really want one!

5 Wow! This old chair is really hard. It _____ like a rock!

4 💬 **Choose five topics from the box. Write sentences using each of the sense verbs. Then compare with your partner.**

| classical music   chocolate milk
new clothes   pizza   the beach
snow   coffee   old trainers |

_____

_____

_____

_____

_____

>> Grammar reference, page 121

 **Culture** ④

1 **After you read** **Read the text on Pupil's Book page 54 again. Tick the foods that the sentences describe.**

	tamales	croquembouches	dumplings
1 People often eat them at weddings.		✓	
2 People make them with very thin dough.			
3 You must boil them in hot water.			
4 There is cream inside them.			
5 You need banana leaves to make them.			
6 They have meat and vegetables inside them.			

2 **Answer the questions. Write complete sentences.**

1 When is it traditional to eat *tamales* in Puerto Rico? *It's traditional to eat tamales on special days in Puerto Rico.*

2 What do Puerto Ricans put inside the banana leaves? _____

3 Where do people buy croquembouches? _____

4 What is a croquembouche decorated with? _____

5 When do Chinese families make boiled dumplings? _____

6 When do Chinese people celebrate the New Year? _____

3 (4.14) **Listen to a report about a traditional food. Complete the notes.**

Country: ¹ _____ *Vietnam* _____

Food: *Bahn chung* is a sticky rice ² _____ that people eat at New Year.

Recipe:

- ³ _____ rice with meat and yellow mung ⁴ _____.
- Make into ⁵ _____ square cakes.
- Wrap the cakes in ⁶ _____ leaves ⁷ _____ the *bahn chung* in hot water for six hours.

Other facts:

- Some people make *bahn chung* without ⁸ _____.
- People usually eat *bahn chung* with ⁹ _____.

4 📶 **Work in groups. Choose a different traditional festival and find answers to the questions. Write about the festival. Then make a poster about it.**

1 Why do people celebrate this festival?

2 When do people celebrate it?

3 What is a traditional food that people eat?

4 Who makes the food?

5 How do people make the food?

English in action
Offering to help

1 (4.17) **Read and complete the dialogue. Then listen and check.**

> a Chicken with rice and vegetables.   b ~~Yes, please. You can clear the table.~~
>   c How about loading the dishwasher?   d Yes, of course.
>   e I've already washed them.   f Thank you.

Girl: Can I help you with anything, Dad?

Dad: ¹ *b Yes, please. You can clear the table.*

Girl: Do you want me to help cook, too?

Dad: ² _____

Girl: What's for lunch?

Dad: ³ _____

Girl: That sounds delicious. I'll boil the rice.

Dad: ⁴ _____

Girl: Shall I chop the vegetables, too?

Dad: Yes, please. ⁵ _____

Girl: What do you want me to do now?

Dad: ⁶ _____

2 ✳ **Read the sentences. Write offers. Then act out the dialogues with your partner.**

1 'I have a test tomorrow.'

  I'll help you study for it.

2 'The kitchen is a mess!'

  Do you _____?

3 'I didn't have lunch today.'

  Can I _____?

4 'We don't have any milk.'

  Shall I _____?

5 'I'm tidying the garage.'

  What do _____?

6 'The floor isn't very clean.'

  I'll _____.

Pronunciation

3 (4.18) 💬 **Listen and read.**
Do the questions go up or down?
Draw an up arrow (↗) or a down
arrow (↘) . Then practise with
your partner.

1 Do you want me to load the
   dishwasher?

2 When can you help me tidy up?

3 What do you want me to clean?

4 Shall I put away my clothes now?

5 Can you please sweep the floor?

6 Who's going to do the washing-up?

Literacy: recipes (4)

Reading

Words in context

1 Unscramble the words and complete the sentences.

1 I don't have a metal _____tray_____ (yart) so I can't bake cheese straws.
2 John always puts hot chocolate _____ (eacus) on his ice cream.
3 Would you like some _____ (retubt) in your sandwich?
4 You'll only need one _____ (snopateo) of salt for this recipe.
5 We need a _____ (logriln nip) to make the pizza dough very thin.
6 My grandma always has _____ (carme) and sugar in her coffee.

2 Read the recipe for fruit sticks on Pupil's Book page 56 again. Number the instructions in order.

[ ] a After that, melt the chocolate in the microwave.
[ ] b Then take the fruit and chop it into small pieces.
[ ] c Next, heat the chocolate and cream and mix them again.
[1] d First, be sure you have all the ingredients.
[ ] e Then add the cream to the chocolate and mix them.
[ ] f Finally, eat the fruit with the hot chocolate sauce.

3 Read the recipe for cheese straws again. Answer the questions. Write complete sentences.

1 How much cheese do we need to make this recipe?
We need 75 grammes of cheese to make this recipe.

2 What must we beat before we add it to the other ingredients?
_____

3 Why do we need to rub the butter with our fingers?
_____

4 What do we do after we roll the dough with a rolling pin?
_____

5 What must we do with the long pieces of dough?
_____

6 How hot must the oven be to cook the dough?
_____

4 Work in groups. Choose a dinner recipe. Discuss the questions and make notes. Then share your ideas with the class.

1 Why do you like the recipe so much?
2 What things do you need to make it?
3 How must you prepare the recipe?
4 How does the food smell and taste?

Writing

1 **Number the pictures in order. Then complete the recipe.**

after that   finally   ~~first~~   next   then

a	b	c	d	e
☐	☐	1	☐	☐

Hot tomato and cheese sandwiches

- _____ *First* _____ , cut some thin pieces of tomato and cheese.
- _____ , put the tomato on a piece of bread.
- _____ , add the cheese and another piece of bread.
- _____ , put butter on the outside of the sandwich.
- _____ , cook the sandwich very slowly on both sides.

tip **Writing**

When you write instructions, make sure the order is clear. You can use bullet points (•), numbers (1, 2, 3, etc.), and words like *first*, *next*, *then*.

2 **Plan a recipe for a dish that you like.**

Write a title for your recipe. →

List the ingredients you need for your recipe.
Use abbreviations: *g (grammes)*, *ml (millilitres)*, *ºC (degrees Celsius)*, etc. →

List the recipe instructions. Use cooking verbs: *add, cut, chop, boil*, etc. →

3 **Now write your recipe.**

4 **Check your work. Tick (✓) the steps when you have done them.**

Have I listed all the recipe ingredients? ☐   Have I used cooking verbs? ☐

Have I used abbreviations correctly? ☐   Have I written a clear sequence of instructions? ☐

1 Complete the phrases for jobs at home.

1 l*oad the dishwasher*
2 s_____
3 w_____
4 t_____
5 d_____
6 t_____
7 e_____
8 v_____

2 Complete the texts with cooking words.

Please can you lay the table? We need six
[1] k*nives*_____, six [2] f_____ and
six [3] s_____. We don't need any
[4] c_____ today because we aren't
having Chinese food. Don't forget the
[5] s_____ and [6] p_____.

First you [7] c_____ potatoes into tiny
pieces. Then you [8] b_____ them in
water. After that, you [9] m_____ the
potatoes with butter and [10] a_____ a
teaspoon of salt. Next, [11] c_____ some
cheese and put it on top. [12] B_____ in
the oven for 20 minutes at 180°C.

3 Write Present perfect sentences.

1 make / I / already / dinner   *I've already made dinner.*
2 just / watch / film / a / he   _____
3 stop / not / raining / yet / it   _____
4 finish / we / our / already / homework _____
5 yet / she / not / me / call   _____

4 Complete the sentences with the sense verbs.

1 Those flowers ____*look*____ so pretty.
They're a beautiful colour.

2 That _____ pop music. It's my
favourite kind of music.

3 Yum! This cake _____ delicious! Can I
have another slice, please?

4 This sweater _____ wool. It's really
soft.

5 Yuck! The kitchen bin _____ horrible.

Self-evaluation

5 Answer the questions about your work in Unit 4.

1 How was your work in this unit? Choose. ☐ OK ☐ Good ☐ Excellent

2 Which lesson was your favourite? _____

3 Which parts of the unit were difficult for you? _____

4 What new things can you talk about now? _____

5 How can you work and learn better in the next unit? _____

Get ready for...

A2 Flyers Listening Part 3

Think! **1 Read the task carefully. Make sure you know what you have to do.**

Try! **2 Look at pictures A–H in Activity 3. Match them to the words.**

1 [D] bathroom	2 [ ] bedroom	3 [ ] dining room	4 [ ] garage
5 [ ] garden	6 [ ] hall	7 [ ] kitchen	8 [ ] living room

Do! **3** 4.21 **Which parts of the house are these things in? Listen and write a letter for each thing.**

Exam tip

Check you know the names of what is in the pictures before you listen.

1 backpack [F]

2 tablet [ ]

3 textbook [ ]

4 trainers [ ]

5 dog [ ]

6 guitar [ ]

A

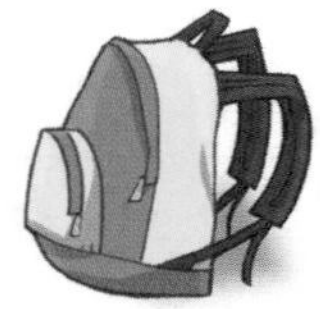

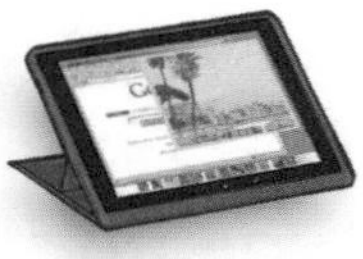

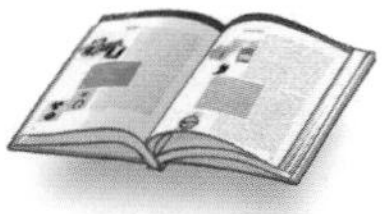

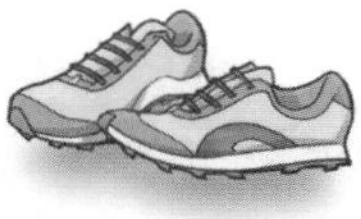

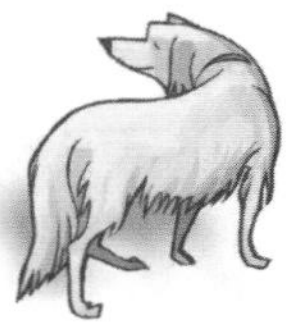

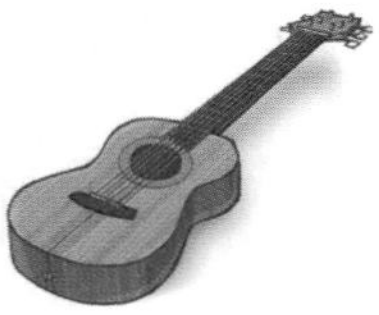

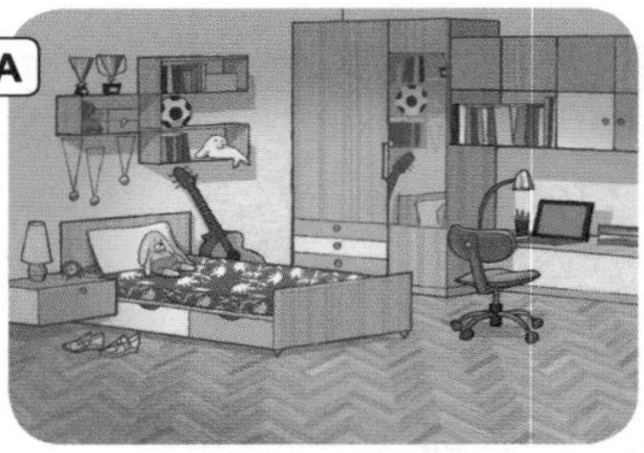

B

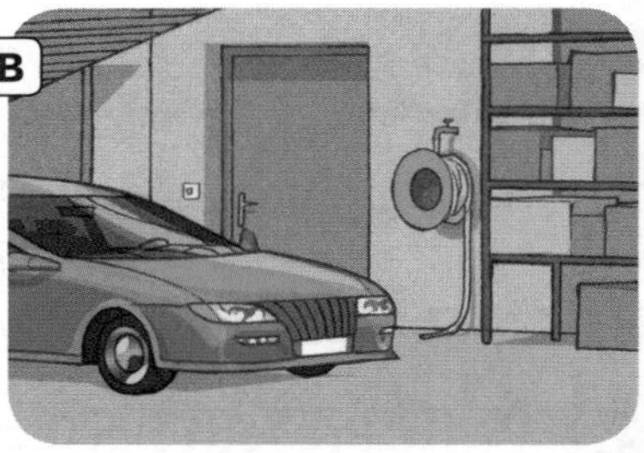

C

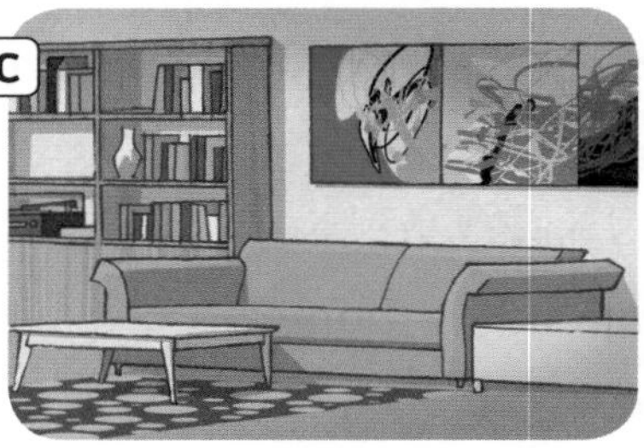

D

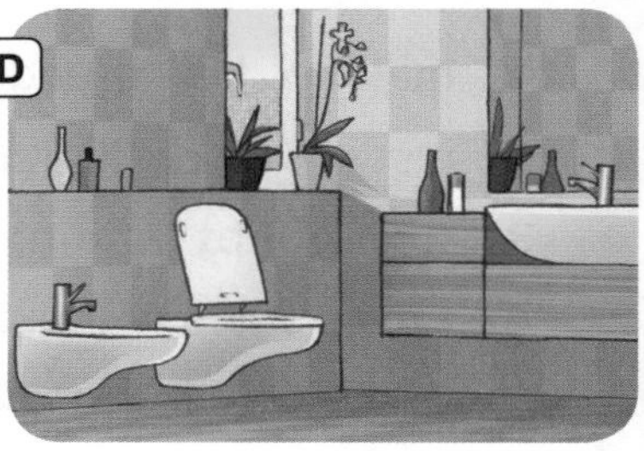

E

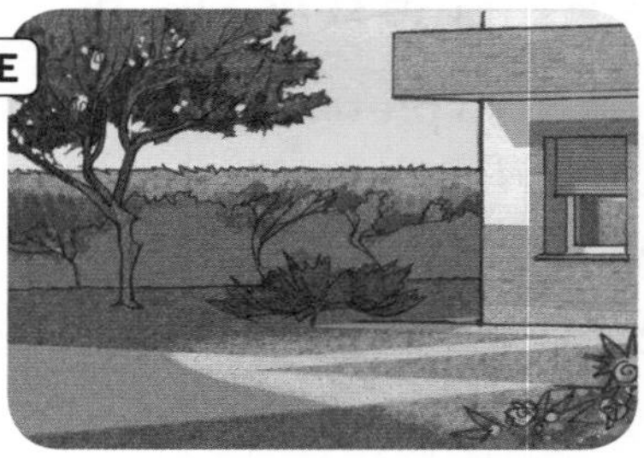

F

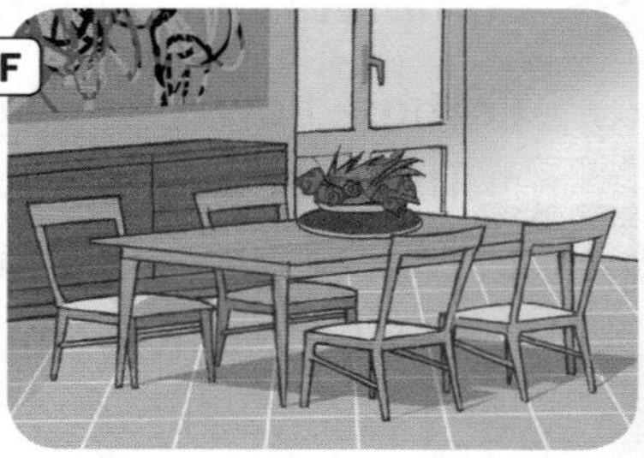

G

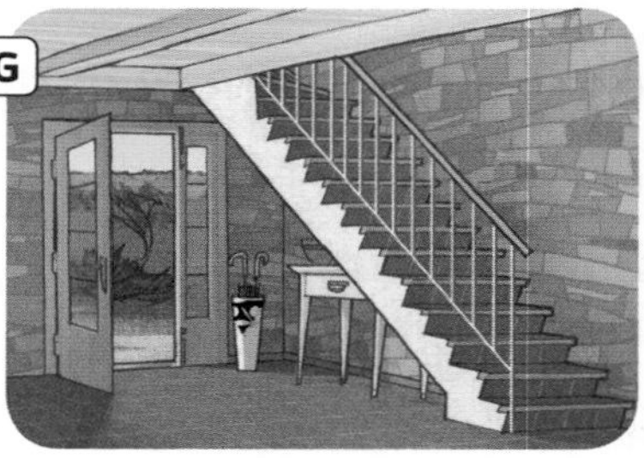

H

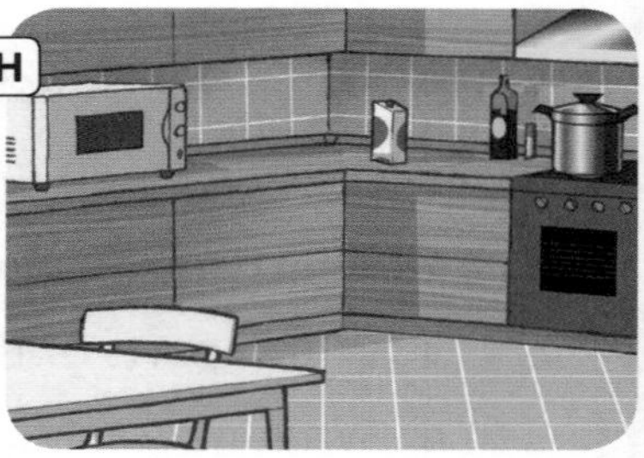

A2 Flyers Reading and Writing Part 5

Think! **1** **Read the task carefully. Make sure you know what you have to do.**

Try! **2** **Make sentences with the same meaning. Write one, two, three or four words.**

1 That's Mark. He's in my class.   Mark is a boy ___who is___ in my class.

2 I was sleeping. You called me.   You called me _____ sleeping.

3 I can't remember the recipe.   I have _____ the recipe.

Do! **3** 🎯 **Look at the picture and read the story. Write one, two, three or four words to complete the sentences.**

> **tip Exam**
> For each gap in the sentence, think of possible words which may fit.

A great birthday!

My name's Jenny. Last Saturday, I celebrated my birthday with a big party. I invited all my friends from school. The weather was cold and it was raining, so we couldn't have the party in the garden. We had to have it in the house. I tidied the living room and then my sister Karen helped me clear the table for all the party food. My brother Michael wanted to be the DJ because he has a great collection of music. My parents prepared all the food. My dad cooked some burgers and my mum baked a big cake with my name on the top. For dessert, we had cake and ice cream and then I opened all my presents. My favourite present was a new smartphone from my parents. I really needed it because my old one was broken. Luckily we have a dishwasher, so we didn't have to do all the washing-up after the party!

Example   Jenny had a big party to ___celebrate her___ birthday.

1 Jenny invited lots _____ from school to her party.

2 They had the party in the house _____ wasn't nice.

3 Jenny _____ living room for the party.

4 Michael has lots of music _____ the DJ.

5 Jenny's parents prepared _____ and a big cake.

6 Jenny's favourite present was a _____ .

7 Jenny and her family didn't have to _____ because they have a dishwasher.

5 Favourite fashions

Vocabulary

1 **Find and write 12 words for describing clothes.**

1 *tight*
2 _____
3 _____
4 _____
5 _____
6 _____
7 _____
8 _____
9 _____
10 _____
11 _____
12 _____

↓	H	I	S	U	D	C	L	E	I	N	A	S	S	P	O	M	P	A	↑
T	S	O	A	A	E	O	B	B	A	S	F	H	E	O	C	F	E	T	↑
I	A	N	C	L	P	M	A	A	L	M	N	I	L	T	N	O	L	T	D
G	F	A	E	S	I	F	T	G	P	A	U	O	B	T	U	R	B	E	E
H	T	B	L	T	R	O	R	G	Y	R	T	N	A	E	D	T	A	R	N

2 **Read and complete the texts with the words in Activity 1.**

Zac's clothes are always modern and
¹ f a s h i o n a b l e. Today
he's wearing his ² _ i _ _ _ _ jeans.
They're ³ _ _ _ _ i _ black. He's also
wearing a ⁴ _ a _ _ e _ _ _ _ _ _
shirt. Zac's clothes look very
⁵ _ _ a _ _ _, but he doesn't like
them. He can't relax in them
because they are so
⁶ _ _ _ o _ _ o _ _ a _ _ e!

Kate isn't into fashion at all. She prefers
wearing ⁷ _ _ a _ u _ _ _ _ clothes. Her
⁸ _ _ _ o _ _ _ e _ sweater is very big
and ⁹ _ _ a _ _ _ _ and her
¹⁰ _ _ _ _ i _ _ _ _ trousers are old.
Kate knows that her clothes are
¹¹ u _ _ _ a _ _ _ _ o _ _ _ _ _ e,
but that isn't important to her
because they're also very
¹² _ o _ _ o _ _ a _ _ _!

3 **Read the *I'm learning* box. Then read and complete the phrases.**

I'm learning

Using new and recycled words
A good way to practise new words is to
use them with words you already know.
New: *striped*
Review: *T-shirt*

I have a striped T-shirt.

1 _____*baggy*_____ jeans
2 a _____ dress
3 _____ shoes
4 a _____ scarf
5 _____ shorts
6 an _____ shirt

[1] [2] [3] [4]

[5] [6]

4 **Write three or more sentences about your own clothes and style. Use words for clothes from this lesson and other words you already know.**

 **Team Talk** 5

1 (5.4) **Listen and read the dialogue on Pupil's Book page 62 again. Then complete the sentences.**

> cheaper   comfortable   different   fun   important   ~~unfashionable~~

I think our school uniform is boring and
¹ _unfashionable_ .
I'd like to look
² _____ from other people at my school. I really want to wear clothes that are more ³ _____ .

I think uniforms are smart and
⁴ _____ .
Did you also know that uniforms are
⁵ _____
to buy than other clothes? I think that's really
⁶ _____ .

2 **Answer the questions. Write complete sentences.**

1 Why does Bobby like dressing the same as other students? _He likes being part of a team._
2 What kind of skirt does Lara want to wear to school? _____
3 Why does Bobby say to Lara, 'Not together, I hope!' _____
4 What does Lara say about the uniform trousers? _____
5 Who should look at Lara's new ideas for the uniform? _____
6 How will Lara's design be different from the old uniform? _____

3 (5.5) **Read and complete the dialogues with the correct expressions. Then listen and check.**

> I guess so. × 2   I hope. × 2   Come on! × 2

1 **A:** This jacket doesn't look good on me.
   B: ¹ _Come on!_ It looks great. The colour looks really good on you.
   A: ² _____ And I can wear it with my new jeans.
   B: How much is it?
   A: Not too much, ³ _____ I don't have a lot of money!

2 **A:** Are you going to Tom's party?
   B: ⁴ _____ But I'm angry.
   A: Not with me, ⁵ _____
   B: No! I'm angry because I don't have anything to wear.
   A: ⁶ _____ You have lots of nice clothes.

4 **Work in pairs. Write another dialogue for each expression. Then act out the dialogues.**

Grammar

too and not ... enough

1 🎧 5.8 **Listen and complete.**

> comfortable enough   long enough
> nice enough   tight enough   too casual
> too plain   ~~too old~~   too small

Kyra is giving away some clothes that are
¹ _____too old_____ for her. Maddie
sees a sweatshirt and says it looks
² _____ to wear. Kyra tells Maddie
the sweatshirt isn't ³_____ and it's
also ⁴_____ for her. Then Maddie
sees a scarf. It isn't ⁵_____ for
Kyra now, but Maddie doesn't want the
scarf because it's ⁶_____. Finally,
Maddie sees some boots. They aren't
⁷_____ for Kyra.
She says they aren't ⁸_____.

2 **Read and complete the sentences with an adjective and *too* or *not ... enough*.**

1 These jeans should be tighter. They're
   _____too baggy_____ for me.

2 I can't wear this casual dress tonight. It
   isn't _____ for a party.

3 These shoes are _____. I want
   something more patterned.

4 Oh dear! This T-shirt costs 100 euros!
   That's much _____ for me!

5 My new shoes aren't _____.
   I prefer my old trainers.

6 The weather is quite cool today. I don't
   think it's _____ to wear
   shorts and a T-shirt.

3 **What's wrong? Look and write sentences with *too* and *not ... enough*.**

shoes / big
Her shoes are too big.

T-shirt / long
_____

sweater / baggy
_____

clothes / warm
_____

glasses / fashionable
_____

trousers / short
_____

4 **Write six sentences about clothes you don't wear very often. Use the words below and *too* or *not ... enough*.**

> fashionable   tight   uncomfortable
> plain   baggy   smart   unfashionable
> comfortable   casual   patterned

1 *My black jeans are too tight.*
2 _____
3 _____
4 _____
5 _____
6 _____

5 💬 **Compare your sentences from Activity 4 with your partner. Do you have similar answers? Write their sentences in your notebook.**

>> **Grammar reference, page 122**

WOW! Book Club ⑤

1 `After you read` **Remember the words to complete the sentences. Read the story on Pupil's Book page 64 again and check.**

1 Princess Priscilla had lots of __clothes__ and games, but she was _____.

2 She had an _____. She took off the _____ and ran down the stairs.

3 'Buy my _____,' said a man. 'They're made of _____.'

4 'I'd like these _____,' she said, 'and you can _____ this dress'.

5 She tried on some _____ leggings, a _____ sweatshirt and some trainers.

6 Later at the _____, the king and queen didn't _____ their daughter.

2 **Read the sentences. Write *T* (true), *F* (false) or *DS* (doesn't say). Explain your answers.**

1 The princess noticed the date when she was playing games.

[F] *She noticed the date when she was looking at her diary.*

2 The princess didn't think her clothes and her crown were fashionable.

[ ]

3 An Italian woman was selling some leather shoes.

[ ]

4 Priscilla sold some comfortable leggings at the shop.

[ ]

5 The children who talked to Priscilla didn't go to her school.

[ ]

6 The king and queen were surprised when they saw Priscilla.

[ ]

3 **Read the *Work with words* box. Then write the opposites of the adjectives.**

> **Work with words**
>
> **The negative prefix *un-***
>
> We can use the negative prefix *un-* to make the opposites of some adjectives.
> comfortable → **un**comfortable

1 exciting _*unexciting*_ **4** kind _____

2 fashionable _____ **5** safe _____

3 happy _____ **6** tidy _____

4 **Use the negative adjectives from Activity 3 to write sentences with the same meaning.**

1 The living room is messy. *The living room is untidy.*

2 Those boots aren't fashionable. _____

3 Today was a boring day. _____

4 I was sad when I lost my phone. _____

5 Don't be mean to other people! _____

6 Don't play in dangerous places. _____

5 💡 **Write six sentences. Use the words with negative prefixes in Activity 3 or any other words with negative prefixes you know.**

1 **Read and complete the crossword.**

```
        1
        G
        L
    2   O
        V     4
    3   E
        S           5
6
7
```

1 You wear them on your hands.
2 A king or queen wears it on their head.
3 It keeps your trousers up.
4 They cover your legs and your feet.
5 You use this to tell the time.
6 You wear it on your head in cold weather.
7 They cover your legs, but not your feet.

2 🎧 (5.12) **Listen to two conversations. Write 1 or 2 next to the clothes items you hear. There are three clothes items you do not need.**

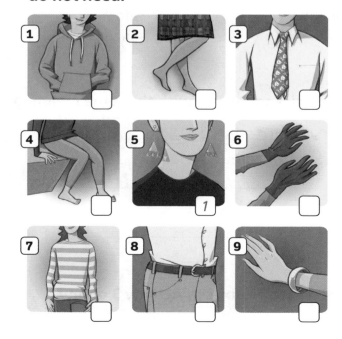

Present passive

3 **Read and complete the sentences with the Present passive.**

1 That blue cotton fabric ___is called___ (call) denim.
2 My new shoes _____ (make) of leather.
3 Earrings _____ (wear) by lots of people.
4 The kitchen _____ (clean) every day.
5 Baked potatoes _____ (cook) in an oven.
6 Wool _____ (use) for making warm clothes.

4 **Look and write about how we make tomato sauce for pizza. Use the Present passive.**

| clean | use | send | make | ~~pick~~ |

1 _The tomatoes are picked._
2 _____
3 _____
4 _____
5 _____

5 💡 **Write five sentences about things you have at home. What are they made of? What are they used for? Use the words in the box or your own ideas.**

| cotton gold leather metal paper |
| plastic rubber silver wool |

>> Grammar reference, page 122

1 `After you read` **Read the text on Pupil's Book page 66 again. Tick (✓) the correct country.**

	Scotland	Guatemala	Kenya
1 The festival of Todos Santos is celebrated here.		✓	
2 Traditional kilts are worn by men and boys.			
3 Bracelets and earrings are worn by many people.			
4 Clothes are made from special tartan fabric.			
5 Traditional dancing is done by girls.			
6 Striped shirts are worn by men and boys.			

2 **Answer the questions. Write complete sentences.**

1 When are traditional clothes worn?

Traditional clothes are worn at festivals and celebrations.

2 What is Scottish tartan fabric usually made of?

_____

3 What musical instrument is traditionally played in Scotland?

_____

4 What do traditional Todos Santos clothes look like?

_____

5 What do Guatemalan boys watch at the Todos Santos festival?

_____

6 What is worn on Samburu girls' arms?

_____

3 (5.14) **Listen to a presentation about traditional clothes. Complete the notes.**

Clothes: ^{1} ___*hanbok*___   **Country:** ^{2} _____

Special occasions: ^{3} _____ and weddings

Usually made of: cotton or ^{4} _____

Women's clothes: ^{5} _____ skirt and ^{6} _____ jacket

Men's clothes: ^{7} _____ shirt and jacket, and ^{8} _____ trousers

4 📶 **Work in groups. Choose one of the traditional costumes in the box and find answers to the questions. Write about your costume. Then make a factfile about it.**

Indian sari   Japanese kimono   Moroccan djellaba

1 What do the clothes look like?
2 When are the clothes worn?

3 Who are the clothes worn by?
4 What are the clothes made of?

English in action
Shopping for clothes

1 (5.17) **Read and complete the dialogue. Then listen and check.**

> **a** Can I try them on?   **b** And do you sell silk tops?   **c** I'm looking for some shorts.
> **d** Can I help you?   **e** The changing room is over there.   **f** Do you have this one in blue?

Shop assistant:	Good morning. ¹d Can I help you? _____
Girl:	Yes, please. ² _____
Shop assistant:	The shorts are over there, next to the mirror.
Girl:	Great, thanks. ³ _____
Shop assistant:	Yes, we do. What size do you need?
Girl:	Medium, please. ⁴ _____
Shop assistant:	Of course. ⁵ _____
Girl:	Great. ⁶ _____
Shop assistant:	Yes, we do, but we don't have any at the moment.
Girl:	Oh, that's OK.

2 ☀ **Imagine you're in a clothes shop. Write your answers to the questions. Use the dialogue in Activity 1 to help you. Then act out the dialogue with your partner.**

1 Can I help you?

I'm looking for ... _____

2 What colour would you like?

_____

3 What size do you need?

_____

4 Would you like to try it/them on?

_____

5 Can I get you anything else?

_____

Pronunciation

3 💬 (5.18) **Listen and read. Circle** ⟨able⟩ **if it is stressed and underline** _able_ **if it isn't stressed. Then practise with your partner.**

1 This sweatshirt is too baggy. It isn't suit_able_.

2 I'm wearing comfortable trainers.

3 Please can you clear the table?

4 My parents like growing vegetables.

5 Have you seen the new school timetable?

6 I love your fashionable trousers.

7 Let's sit at this picnic table.

8 Oh, no! My new tie isn't washable.

Reading

1   **Read and complete the sentences.**

| crazy | rich | light | heavy | ~~pointed~~ | normal |

1   I don't like those _____*pointed*_____ shoes. Do you have any rounded ones?

2   Tom's parents drive an expensive sports car. Are they _____?

3   I can't carry this big box. It's too _____ for me. What's in it?

4   Lisa's wearing a long, wool dress in August! Is she _____?

5   I hate wearing a school uniform. I'd rather wear _____ clothes!

6   Silk is a great fabric for summer clothes. It's very _____ and cool.

2   **Read the text on Pupil's Book page 68 again. Which clothes items do these sentences describe? There could be more than one correct answer.**

1   Only very rich men could wear them.   _____*wigs*_____

2   They were very long and pointed.   _____

3   Some of them were wider than doors.   _____

4   They could make people look taller.   _____

5   It wasn't easy to move around in them.   _____

6   The king of France liked wearing these.   _____

3   **Read the text again. Answer the questions. Write complete sentences.**

1   Why did some people in the past wear strange clothes?
They wore strange clothes because they
wanted to be fashionable.

2   Who bought wigs after the French king started wearing one?
_____
_____

3   Why was it difficult for women to get around in whalebone dresses?
_____
_____

4   How are dresses today different from the dresses in the text?
_____
_____

5   Why were chopines probably useful on wet, rainy days?
_____
_____

6   How much longer were crakowes than normal shoes for men?
_____
_____

4   **Work in groups. Think about strange fashions in your country. Discuss the questions and make notes. Then share your ideas with the class.**

1   What strange clothes do people wear?

2   What is strange about these clothes?

3   Who wears these strange clothes?

4   Why do some people like wearing them?

5   Do you wear strange clothes? Why? Why not?

Writing

1 **Read the sentences. Then write them as one sentence with commas.**

1 Emily has long hair. It's also curly.

Emily has long, curly hair.

2 I bought a comfortable jacket. It's washable too.

_____

3 Paul and Tom were wearing traditional kilts. They were woollen.

_____

4 The princess had a beautiful crown. It was gold.

_____

5 You should wear some smart trousers. They should be black.

_____

6 We saw a long film last night. It was boring.

_____

> **tip** **Writing**
>
> Use a comma when you have two adjectives together before a noun:
> *long, curly hair*
> *big, heavy dresses*
> But be careful:
> *Crakowes were long and pointed.*

2 **Plan an information text about a traditional costume from your country.**

Write a title.	→ _____
Write a short introduction. Give basic information.	→ _____
Include pictures. They can be photos or drawings.	→ _____
Add captions to pictures to give more information.	→ _____
Add labels to the pictures.	→ _____

3 **Now write your information text.**

4 **Check your work. Tick (✓) the steps when you have done them.**

Have I described the costume well? ☐

Have I used *too* and *not … enough* correctly? ☐

Have I used the Present passive correctly? ☐

Have I used commas correctly? ☐

1 **Circle the adjectives. Then look and write sentences to describe the clothes items.**

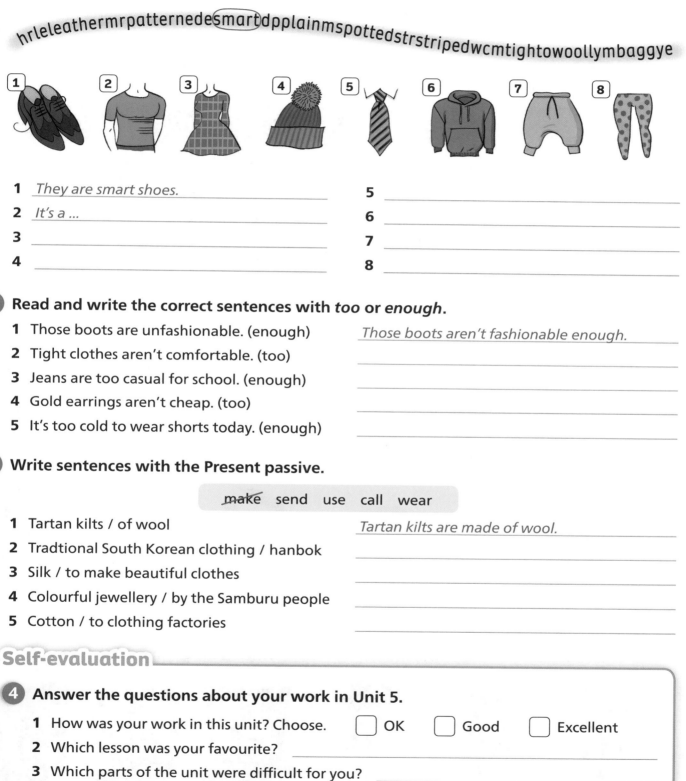

hrleleathermrpatternede(smart)dpplainmspottedstrstripedwcmtightowoollymbaggye

1 *They are smart shoes.*

2 *It's a ...*

3 _____

4 _____

5 _____

6 _____

7 _____

8 _____

2 **Read and write the correct sentences with *too* or *enough*.**

1 Those boots are unfashionable. (enough)   *Those boots aren't fashionable enough.*

2 Tight clothes aren't comfortable. (too)   _____

3 Jeans are too casual for school. (enough)   _____

4 Gold earrings aren't cheap. (too)   _____

5 It's too cold to wear shorts today. (enough)   _____

3 **Write sentences with the Present passive.**

make   send   use   call   wear

1 Tartan kilts / of wool   *Tartan kilts are made of wool.*

2 Tradtional South Korean clothing / hanbok   _____

3 Silk / to make beautiful clothes   _____

4 Colourful jewellery / by the Samburu people   _____

5 Cotton / to clothing factories   _____

Self-evaluation

4 **Answer the questions about your work in Unit 5.**

1 How was your work in this unit? Choose.   ☐ OK   ☐ Good   ☐ Excellent

2 Which lesson was your favourite? _____

3 Which parts of the unit were difficult for you? _____

4 What new things can you talk about now? _____

5 How can you work and learn better in the next unit? _____

Get ready for...

A2 Flyers Listening Part 4 / A2 Key for Schools Listening Part 1

Think! **1** Read the task carefully. Make sure you know what you have to do.

Try! **2** (5.21) Which shirt does the boy like? Listen and tick (✓) the correct picture. Then explain your answer.

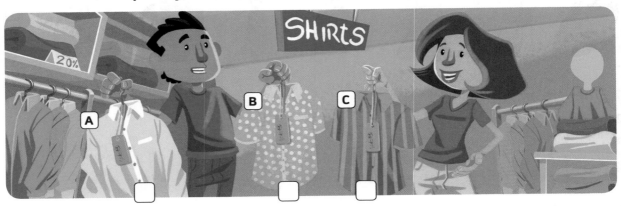

Do! **3** (5.22) Listen. For each question, choose the correct answer.

tip **Exam**
Remember to focus on the key information that you hear.

1 What is the boy going to wear to the party?

A ☐   B ☐   C ☐

2 What does the girl's uniform look like?

A ☐   B ☐   C ☐

3 What did the boy buy for his mum?

A ☐   B ☐   C ☐

4 When is the girl meeting her friends?

A ☐   B ☐   C ☐

A2 Key for Schools Reading and Writing Part 1

Think! **1** Read the task carefully. Make sure you know what you have to do.

Try! **2** Read the message. Choose the correct answer. Then explain your answer.

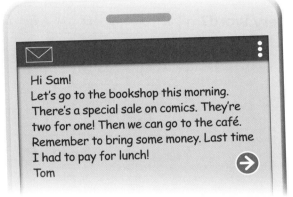

Hi Sam!
Let's go to the bookshop this morning. There's a special sale on comics. They're two for one! Then we can go to the café. Remember to bring some money. Last time I had to pay for lunch!
Tom

A Tom bought two comic books today.

B All the comic books are cheaper today.

C Sam always forgets his money.

_____

_____

_____

tip **Exam**

Remember to compare each text with each answer option before choosing your answer.

Do! **3** 🎯 For each question, choose the correct answer. Choose A, B or C.

Big Winter Sale!
ALL OF OUR WINTER JACKETS ARE
30% off!
Buy any two woolly hats **for only £10**
Half-price on all leather gloves

A Every jacket in the store is on sale.

B You can buy one woolly hat for £5.

C The shop sells some items made of leather.

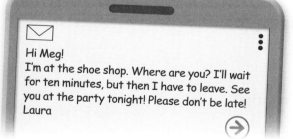

Hi Meg!
I'm at the shoe shop. Where are you? I'll wait for ten minutes, but then I have to leave. See you at the party tonight! Please don't be late!
Laura

A Meg's going to the party in ten minutes.

B Meg's waiting for Laura at the shoe shop.

C Meg thinks Laura is never on time.

This weekend only at Memorial Park
Adults £5
and
students under 16 free
Don't miss it!
SPRING Fashion Fair

A Students don't have to buy tickets.

B The fashion fair is on every weekend.

C The fair is an indoor event.

Adventures

Vocabulary

1 **Read and complete the puzzle. What's the mystery word?**

1 You find this in a first-aid kit. It's long and thin.

2 You can put on you at night when you feel cold.

3 You use this when you want to cut something.

4 You use this when you're lost. It points north.

5 You use these when you want to start a fire.

6 You can sleep in this when the weather is wet.

1	B	A	N	D	A	G	E
2						E	
3		E					
4					A		
5		A					
6						E	

The mystery word is _____.

2 **Read and complete the sentences. Then match.**

1 Ouch! Oh, dear! I think I need a ___plaster___ for my finger. That really hurts!

2 We can cook our dinner on the _____. We don't need to start a fire.

3 Did you pack the _____? We'll need it if someone has an accident.

4 We didn't bring any _____ with us, so we can't go rock climbing.

5 I should buy a new _____ to carry my things. This one's really old.

6 You should bring a _____. The ground is very hard and cold.

3 **Read the *I'm learning* box. Then write sentences about the pairs of objects. How are they similar?**

> **I'm learning**
>
> **Making comparisons**
> You can learn and remember the words for similar things by comparing them.

1 plaster / bandage _____

2 camping stove / campfire _____

3 map / compass _____

4 shelter / tent _____

5 knife / penknife _____

6 sleeping mat / blanket _____

4 **Write three or more sentences comparing other similar things. Use the ideas in the box or your own ideas.**

> boots and shoes   comics and magazines   mobile phones and tablets
> necklace and bracelet   oven and cooker   swimming pool and sports centre

Team Talk 6

1 (6.4) **Read the dialogue on Pupil's Book page 74 again. Complete the sentences. Who said them? Write. Then listen and check.**

bottles   dirty   ~~happy~~   hiking   map   warmer

1 ___Arlo___   I'm so ___happy___ to be going home.
2 _____   Everything in my rucksack is _____ and wet.
3 _____   We had our water _____, but they were empty.
4 _____   Someone saw a river on the _____ so we went to find water.
5 _____   He was wearing _____ boots, but he didn't have waterproof trousers!
6 _____   And next time I go camping, I'll go somewhere that's _____!

2 **Read the dialogue again and circle T (true) or F (false). Explain your answers.**

1 The team had a compass, but no one had a map.   T /(F)
  They had a map, but no one had a compass.

2 They were thirsty and they didn't have anything to drink.   T / F
  _____

3 Arlo fell in the water when he was trying to get some water.   T / F
  _____

4 Mr Barret threw a rope to the person who was in the water.   T / F
  _____

5 Bobby had something to eat after the accident.   T / F
  _____

6 Someone took an embarrassing photo of Lara.   T / F
  _____

3 (6.5) **Read and complete the dialogues with the correct expressions. Then listen and check.**

(Poor you!) × 2   (How embarrassing!) × 2   (What an adventure!) × 2

1 **A:** You're wearing two different shoes.
  B: Oh, dear! ___How embarrassing!___

2 **A:** I'm going camping in the Sahara desert!
  B: Lucky you! _____

3 **A:** I'm really sad. I've lost my mobile phone.
  B: _____ Was it very new?

4 **A:** Carla's on holiday in the Amazon.
  B: Really? _____

5 **A:** Tom fell in the pool during the party.
  B: Oh, no. _____

6 **A:** I can't do my Science project. It's too difficult!
  B: _____ Can I help?

4 **Work in pairs. Write another dialogue for each expression. Then act out the dialogues.**

Grammar

Indefinite pronouns

1 🔊 **(6.8) Read and complete the sentences with the correct indefinite pronouns. Then listen and check.**

1 Do you know _____*anyone*_____ who has a tent?

2 Sam needs _____ to put under his sleeping bag.

3 The shop's closed, so there's _____ to buy food.

4 I can't put _____ in that rucksack. It's too small.

5 Is there _____ we can go for a nice dinner?

6 We can't go climbing because _____ brought any rope.

2 Look at the picture. Read and write sentences with indefinite pronouns.

1 There's _____*no one*_____ in the shelter. They've gone hiking today.

2 There's _____ in the blanket, but we can't see it.

3 _____ is on the floor because there isn't any furniture.

4 _____ has brought some rope to go mountain climbing.

5 There's _____ to wash. You must do that in the river.

6 There isn't _____ in the first-aid kit. It's empty.

3 Read and underline the incorrect indefinite pronouns. Then write the correct sentences.

1 I want to live <u>everywhere</u> interesting, like Paris.
I want to live somewhere interesting, like Paris.

2 Oh dear. There's anything to eat in the fridge.
_____

3 I think everything will have fun at the picnic.
_____

4 You don't need to bring nothing to the party.
_____

5 Where's my bag? I've looked for it anywhere!
_____

6 I know anyone who could help you study.
_____

4 💡 Read the questions. Then write true answers for you.

1 Is there anywhere you would like to go on holiday?
_____
_____

2 Would you like to go camping somewhere?
_____
_____

3 Do you know anyone who likes hiking?
_____
_____

4 Is there anything you like doing outdoors?
_____
_____

5 💬 Work with your partner. Ask them the questions from Activity 4 and write their answers in your notebook.

Grammar reference, page 123

1 **After you read** Read the adventure story on Pupil's Book page 76 again. Then number the events in order.

- [ ] **a** Dad and Sammy found Hannah in the snow after an accident.
- [ ] **b** They decided to ski back to the village through the forest.
- [ ] **c** Sammy offered to get help while Dad stayed with Hannah.
- [ ] **d** Hannah thanked her brother and said she was sorry.
- [1] **e** Hannah and her family were at a café in the mountains.
- [ ] **f** A rescue team came to take Hannah back to the village.
- [ ] **g** Hannah started skiing without putting on her helmet.

2 Answer the questions. Use complete sentences.

1 What was Hannah doing at the café before the accident?

She was drinking hot chocolate with her father and brother.

2 Why did Dad think it was OK to ski back through the forest?

_____

3 Why did Hannah tell her brother that he was a baby?

_____

4 How badly was Hannah hurt in the skiing accident?

_____

5 Why didn't Dad call someone for help on his phone?

_____

6 What did the rescuers use to take Hannah to the village?

_____

3 Read the *Work with words* box. Then complete the sentences with the collocations with *keep*.

Work with words

Collocations: *keep* + adjective
We can use adjectives after the verb *keep* for situations that don't change.
*I wear a helmet to **keep safe**.*
We can put an object between the verb and the adjective.
*My helmet **keeps me safe**.*

still   tidy   fit   ~~warm~~   safe   cold   dry

1 Campers need blankets to ___*keep warm*___ .

2 Helmets are good because they _____ you _____.

3 You must do some exercise every day to _____ _____.

4 We have fridges at home to _____ our food _____.

5 When it's raining, you need an umbrella to _____ _____.

6 Don't be messy. You should _____ your bedroom _____.

7 I'm going to take your photo, so please _____ _____.

4 Write five true sentences about you. Use collocations with *keep* from Activity 3 or any other collocations you know.

1 Complete the phrases.

_b_ u _r_ _n_ your hand   _ a _ _ over

_ _ e a _ your arm   _ a _ e an accident

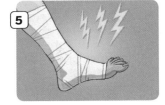

_ u _ _ your ankle   _ u _ your finger

2 🎧 (6.12) **Listen to three conversations. Which two phrases do you hear in each one? Write them in the order you hear them.**

> call an ambulance   ~~have a pain~~
> keep cool   keep warm
> lie down   take medicine

Conversation 1: _have a pain,_ _____

Conversation 2: _____

Conversation 3: _____

should/shouldn't, must/mustn't, need to/don't need to

3 **Read and complete the sentences with the correct form of _should_, _must_ or _need to_.**

1 You ___shouldn't___ stay up late tonight. You'll be tired tomorrow.

2 We _____ speak very quietly when we're in the library.

3 I _____ buy a sandwich. I brought one from home today.

4 Jack's boots are quite old. He _____ buy some new ones.

5 I _____ forget my homework tomorrow. It's very important.

6 You _____ go outdoors more. You're indoors all day.

4 **Read the sentences and write responses. Use the correct form of _should_, _must_ or _need to_.**

1 'I haven't eaten anything today.'
   You should eat something.

2 'I watch a lot of TV every day.'
   _____

3 'I was outside. Now I feel cold.'
   _____

4 'I think I've broken my arm.'
   _____

5 'I brush my teeth six times a day.'
   _____

6 'I use my phone in the cinema.'
   _____

5 💬 **Compare your responses in Activity 4 with your partner. Who wrote the best response?**

>>> Grammar reference, page 123

Culture 6

1 After you read **Read the text on Pupil's Book page 78 again. Then read the comments. Which Scout groups are these people writing about?**

1 'The park was dirty, but we cleaned it up!'   _Scouts in Australia_____

2 'I learned some useful tips for emergencies.'   _____

3 'Now I can make a campfire. That's great!'   _____

4 'Everyone took turns putting on bandages.'   _____

5 'Sleeping in the forest was fun. I loved it.'   _____

6 'We picked up about ten bags of rubbish.'   _____

2 **Answer the questions. Use complete sentences.**

1 What badge are the Scouts in the USA trying to get?

_The Scouts in the USA are trying to get their first-aid badge._____

2 What first-aid situation are the Scouts practising in the photo?

_____

3 Why do Scouts clean up local places?

_____

4 What day are the Australian Scouts celebrating?   _____

5 Where are the English Scouts going to sleep tonight? _____

6 How do Scouts usually cook when they are camping?   _____

3 (6.14) **Listen to a report. Complete the notes.**

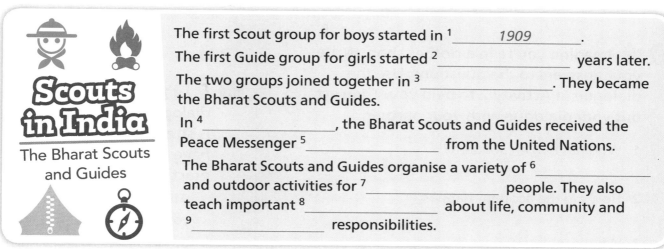

Scouts in India
The Bharat Scouts and Guides

The first Scout group for boys started in [1]_____1909_____.
The first Guide group for girls started [2]_____ years later.
The two groups joined together in [3]_____. They became the Bharat Scouts and Guides.
In [4]_____, the Bharat Scouts and Guides received the Peace Messenger [5]_____ from the United Nations.
The Bharat Scouts and Guides organise a variety of [6]_____ and outdoor activities for [7]_____ people. They also teach important [8]_____ about life, community and [9]_____ responsibilities.

4 🔊 **Work in groups. Find answers to the questions. Write about what you found out. Then share your information with the class.**

1 Who was Robert Baden-Powell?   4 What does a typical Scout uniform include?
2 Where was the scouting camp in 1907?   5 How old must you be to become a Scout?
3 Where and when was the first Scout Rally?

English in action
Asking about injuries and illnesses

1 Read the dialogue on Pupil's Book page 79 again. Answer the questions with *yes* or *no*.

1 Is the girl feeling better? _yes_

2 Has the girl broken anything? _____

3 Has a doctor looked at her ankle? _____

4 Does the girl have a bandage? _____

5 Does the girl have a stomach ache? _____

6 Has she taken any medicine? _____

2 (6.17) Read and complete the dialogue. Then listen and check.

> **a** Have you seen the doctor?   **b** Do you still have a headache?   **c** How's your arm?
> **d** ~~Are you feeling better now?~~   **e** Let's do a puzzle!   **f** Have you cut your hand?

Girl: ¹ _d Are you feeling better now?_

Boy: Yes, thanks. Much better.

Girl: ² _____

Boy: It's OK now, thanks. I haven't broken it!

Girl: That's good! ³ _____

Boy: Yes, I went this afternoon. He put this bandage on it.

Girl: That's good. And what's that plaster for?
⁴ _____

Boy: Yes. I cut it on a piece of glass!

Girl: Oh dear!

Boy: How about you? ⁵ _____

Girl: No, I'm fine now. I took some medicine.

Boy: Great! ⁶ _____

3 ☀ Imagine you're in a clothes shop. Write your answers to the questions. Use the dialogue in Activity 2 to help you. Then act out your dialogue with your partner.

1 Who has had an accident?

_____

2 How did the accident happen?

_____

3 What problem(s) does the person have?

_____

4 Has the person seen a doctor yet?

_____

5 Does the other person have a problem, too?

_____

Pronunciation

4 💬 (6.18) Listen and read the dialogues. Circle (have) if it is stressed and underline *have* if it isn't stressed. Then practise with your partner.

1 A: Have you ever broken your arm?

B: Yes, I have. It really hurt!

2 A: Have you had a cold this year?

B: Yes, I have, and it was terrible.

Words in context

1 **Read and complete the sentences.**

emergency spring blood berries bushes ~~tree trunk~~

1 My cat climbed up that ____tree trunk____. Now it can't get back down.

2 My grandad planted some new trees and _____ in the garden.

3 This water is safe. It came from a natural _____ in the mountains.

4 You shouldn't eat those red _____. They could be dangerous.

5 When there's a serious _____, you should always call for help.

6 My parents give _____ at the hospital to help other people.

2 **Read the quiz on Pupil's Book page 80 again. Then read the sentences and circle _T_ (true) or _F_ (false). Explain your answers.**

1 Your friend should put a bandage on her cut toe.   T **(F)**

    She should wash her toe in clean water.

2 You can start a fire with a plastic bag and a metal spoon.   T / F

    _____

3 Your friend shouldn't try to stay on his front.   T / F

    _____

4 You shouldn't eat anything if you don't know what it is.   T / F

    _____

5 Rain water and spring water are never good to drink.   T / F

    _____

3 **Answer the questions with your own ideas. Discuss your ideas with your partner.**

1 Why shouldn't you jump into a lake to save a friend?

    It's dangerous for you, because you could also have problems.

2 Why mustn't you drink water from the sea?

    _____

3 Why should you wash a small cut with clean water?

    _____

4 What could happen if you eat strange berries or mushrooms?

    _____

5 What other thing can focus sunlight and start a fire?

    _____

4 **Work in groups. Write six more quiz questions about survival, emergencies or first aid. Write three possible answers for each question. Then test another group with your quiz.**

seventy-three   **73**

Writing

tip Writing
Use different words (*e.g. must, shouldn't, never*) so that people need to read carefully!

1 Complete the quiz with the phrases in the box. Then tick (✓) the correct answer to each quiz question.

> put a bandage on his head   ~~move her arm around~~   take some medicine to help his headache
> have a cool shower   see a doctor about her arm   eat an ice cream

FIRST-AID QUIZ

1. If a friend breaks her arm, she should …
   - a put her arm in hot water. ☐
   - b *move her arm around* ☐
   - c _____ ☐

2. If your body feels too hot, you need to …
   - a drink a glass of water. ☐
   - b _____ ☐
   - c _____ ☐

3. If a friend falls and hurts his head, he must …
   - a go to the hospital about his head. ☐
   - b _____ ☐
   - c _____ ☐

2 💡 Plan a quiz about something that interests you.

Think of interesting questions for your quiz.	→	_____
Write three or four options for each question.	→	_____
Make sure all the options make sense.	→	_____
Make sure it isn't easy to guess the right answer.	→	_____

3 Now write your quiz.

4 Check your work. Tick (✓) the steps when you do them.

Have I chosen a good topic for my quiz? ☐

Have I made sure the answer isn't too easy? ☐

Have I written the questions correctly? ☐

Have I written three or four good answer options? ☐

Review 6

1 Read the sentences. What do they describe?

1 You sleep in this when you go camping. It isn't made of sticks.   _a tent_

2 You keep plasters and bandages in this.   _____

3 You carry all your things in this when you go camping.   _____

4 You sleep on this when you go camping. It's comfortable.   _____

5 You need to use this when you are climbing. It's long and thin.   _____

6 You use this to cook when you go camping. It doesn't have sticks.   _____

2 Match to make phrases for injuries and illnesses.

break call cut
fall have lie keep take

a pain an ambulance down your finger
medicine over warm your arm

1 _break your arm_   5 _____
2 _____   6 _____
3 _____   7 _____
4 _____   8 _____

3 Read and complete the sentences with indefinite pronouns

1 We've eaten _everything_ in the fridge. It's empty!

2 I know _____ who can speak six languages.

3 Did you bring _____ to read?

4 There's _____ to go swimming here.

5 Has _____ told you about the party?

6 I've looked _____ for my penknife, but I can't find it.

7 Please may I have _____ to eat. I'm hungry.

8 I have _____ to wear. My clothes are all dirty.

4 Write sentences with the correct form of should, must or need to.

1 you / always / do your homework   _You must always do your homework._

2 we / shout / at our friends   _____

3 I / wear a uniform to school   _____

4 you / drink / water from the sea   _____

5 we / eat / healthy food   _____

6 they / see a doctor   _____

Self-evaluation

5 Answer the questions about your work in Unit 6.

1 How was your work in this unit? Choose. ☐ OK ☐ Good ☐ Excellent

2 Which lesson was your favourite? _____

3 Which parts of the unit were difficult for you? _____

4 What new things can you talk about now? _____

5 How can you work and learn better in the next unit? _____

Get ready for...

A2 Key for Schools Listening Part 3

Think! **1** Read the task carefully. Make sure you know what you have to do.

Try! **2** (6.20) Listen and choose the correct answer. Then explain your answer.

Tom is going to

   A visit the museum next month.

   B go camping with his friend Paul.

   C join a new activities club.

_____

_____

_____

tip **Exam**

Listen the first time to get the gist and then circle the best answer for each question.

Do! **3** (6.21) **For each question, choose the correct answer. You will hear Robert talking to his mother about a camping trip.**

1 Robert isn't going to take

   A a blanket.

   B a sleeping mat.

   C an extra blanket.

2 Mum asks Robert if he

   A knows how to make a fire.

   B has his new rucksack.

   C has packed any matches.

3 Mr Adams is going to

   A take a first-aid kit.

   B cook all of the food.

   C call the camp leader.

4 Robert wants to

   A ask his Dad a question.

   B learn how to cook.

   C take a camping stove.

5 The campers are planning

   A to collect wood in the forest.

   B to go hiking in the woods.

   C to go swimming in the lake.

A2 Key for Schools Reading and Writing Part 3

 1 Read the task carefully. Make sure you know what you have to do.

 2 Read the questions. Then read the text and <u>underline</u> the key information. Answer the questions.

1 Who is the text about?

_____

2 What is the text about?

_____

3 Who wrote the text?

_____

4 What does Katy do?

_____

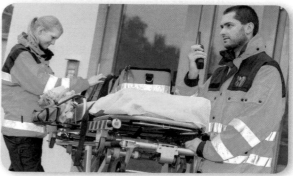

Do! **3** 🎯 **For each question, choose the correct answer.**

> **tip Exam**
> Look at each question carefully and compare each answer option with the text before choosing your answer.

Hello everyone. For this week's blog about jobs, I'm interviewing George Smith. He works as an emergency paramedic in England. It's a difficult job, but it's also quite exciting. George became a paramedic because he wanted to help people who were in trouble. He studied very hard and got his first paramedic job when he was only 26. George started working in a small town, but now he's a paramedic in Manchester, which is a big city. George and his partner Katy must respond quickly when there's an accident. They take turns driving the ambulance. This morning, they helped a woman who had fallen down the stairs at a sports centre. She broke her arm and she also cut her head. George and Katy put a big plaster on the woman's head and then took her to see a doctor at the hospital. After that, they were called to a fire at a fast-food restaurant where they helped a young man. He was one of the waiters and he burned his hand quite badly during the fire. Luckily, no one else was hurt!

1 George became a paramedic
 A to make a lot of money.
 B to have an exciting job.
 C to help people in trouble.
2 How long has George been a paramedic?
 A Since he was 26.
 B For 26 years.
 C Since he finished school.
3 George had his first paramedic job
 A at a hospital in Manchester.
 B in a small town.
 C in a big city.
4 What happened to the woman's arm?
 A She broke it.
 B She cut it.
 C She burned it.
5 The young man hurt his arm
 A when he was cooking.
 B and also cut his head.
 C when he was at work.

Lara's Learning Club

Language booster 2

1 **Read and complete the sentences.**

interesting   recycled   ~~interested~~   comfortable   fashionable   casual

1 Holly is _____*interested*_____ in fashion.
2 _____ clothes make Holly happy.
3 She likes plain, _____ clothes.
4 She sometimes wears a crazy hat because unusual clothes make people _____ .
5 She tries to buy cheap or _____ clothes.
6 Then she changes them so they are more _____ .

2 **Imagine you are a fashion blogger. Answer the questions. Use three or more words.**

1 Who or what made you interested in fashion?

_____ made me interested in fashion.

2 What are your favourite clothes?
My favourite clothes are _____ .

3 Do you often buy new clothes?
_____

4 It's your birthday next week. What are you going to wear to your party? I'm going to wear _____ .

3 **Use words from each column. Write four sentences.**

My brother/sister Music My friends Homework Fashionable clothes	makes make made	me life my mum/dad school	angry. difficult. happy. better. interesting. fun.

1 _____
2 _____
3 _____
4 _____

4 **Write two more sentences about you using make + object + adjective.**

_____
_____

5 **(LB2.3)** **Listen to the dialogue on Pupil's Book page 85 again and circle _T_ (true) or _F_ (false). Explain your answers.**

1 Katy isn't ready yet.   T / F

_____

2 They haven't made a cake yet.   T / F

_____

3 Katy's new dress is casual and patterned.   T / F

_____

4 Katy's jeans aren't baggy enough.   T / F

_____

5 Her jeans make her uncomfortable.   T / F

_____

6 David is wearing smart clothes.   T / F

_____

6 **Circle the clothes in red and the adjectives in blue.**

Dresscomfortablebaggyjeanssweatshirtskirtstripedplaintightssmarttiecasualtighttopleggingscap

7 ✱ **Make a new dialogue. Choose and write clothes on the red lines and adjectives on the blue lines.**

Girl: I don't know what to wear.

Boy: You could wear your new _____
_____ .

Girl: That/Those _____ is/are too _____ .
It/They make/makes me _____ .

Boy: How about your _____ ?

Girl: Yes, OK. I'll wear my _____ _____ .
It's/They're _____ . What are you wearing?

Boy: My _____ _____
and my _____ _____ .
Oh, and this _____ _____
to make it fashionable!

Entertainment

Vocabulary

1 **Write the jobs.**

writer

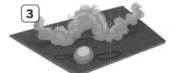

2 **Read and complete the sentences.**

1 This news programme is quite boring and the _____*presenter*_____ isn't very good.

2 Tom's creative and he likes making clothes. He should be a _____.

3 I like watching TV talent shows. Some of the _____ are excellent!

4 J.K. Rowling wrote the Harry Potter books. She's my favourite _____.

5 You're very good at telling funny stories. You would be a great _____.

6 My sister loves gymnastics. She'd like to be a circus _____ one day.

3 **Read the *I'm learning* box. Then write descriptions of the jobs.**

I'm learning

Describing jobs
You can describe jobs by saying what the people do.

An acrobat does acrobatics.
A comedian makes people laugh.

1 An ice skater *dances on ice.* _____

2 A composer _____

3 A bus driver _____

4 A clown _____

5 A costume designer _____

6 A chef _____

4 **Write three or more descriptions of jobs. Use the jobs in the box or your own ideas.**

camera operator   farmer   mechanic   police officer   scientist
waiter   performer   vet   make-up artist

1 (7.4) **Read and complete the sentences from the dialogue on Pupil's Book page 90. Then listen and check.**

body   comedian   cool   funny   funny
~~great~~   man   omelette   on   out   time

1 You're a ____great____ clown, Arlo.

2 Watch _____! We don't want an _____!

3 Very _____, Ting. You should be a _____!

4 That's _____. Is he _____?

5 What do you call a _____ with a big nose and no _____?

6 Come _____, you two! It's _____ for the WOW! Talent Show.

2 **Answer the questions. Write complete sentences.**

1 Why is Arlo's costume a bit small?   *He's had it for a long time.*

2 When did Arlo start to juggle?   _____

3 When did Arlo's uncle become a comedian?   _____

4 When did Arlo see his uncle perform?   _____

5 Why was the answer 'Nobody nose' funny?   _____

3 (7.5) **Read and complete the dialogues with the correct expressions. Then listen and check.**

[I've no idea.] × 2   [That's cool!] × 2   [I get it!] × 2

1 **A:** I'm going to be in the talent show!

B: ¹____*That's cool!*____ What's your talent?

A: Telling jokes! Here's one. What kind of cheese isn't yours?

B: ²_____

A: Nacho cheese! Do you understand?

B: Yes, ³_____ That's terrible!

2 **A:** What time does the talent show start?

B: ⁴_____ No one told me.

A: What are you going to do?

B: I'm going to make people laugh.

A: ⁵_____ So are you a comedian?

B: No, I'm not. I'm a singer!

A: Oh, ⁶_____ That's funny!

4 **Work in pairs. Write another dialogue for each expression. Then act out the dialogues.**

Present perfect with *since* and *for*

1 Read and complete the sentences with *since* or *for*.

1 I've been on the basketball team
   _____*for*_____ two years.

2 We haven't seen Mark _____ last
   Sunday.

3 Tom's played the piano _____ he
   was nine.

4 You've studied English _____
   several years.

5 Ana and Ted have lived in Italy
   _____ 2012.

6 It hasn't rained here _____ a
   long time.

2 (7.8) **Listen and read. Then circle *T* (true) or *F* (false). Explain your answers.**

1 She's been at the café for
   two hours.   **T /(F)**

   She's been at the café for half an hour.

2 He's lived in Manchester since
   he was six.   **T / F**
   _____

3 She hasn't seen Paul since
   last Christmas.   **T / F**
   _____

4 He's known Amy for two weeks. **T / F**
   _____

5 She's wanted to visit Paris
   since she was little.   **T / F**
   _____

3 Write survey questions with *How long* and the Present perfect.

1 you / well / in this town
   How long have you lived in this town?

2 you / be / a student
   _____

3 you / study / English
   _____

4 you / have / a mobile phone
   _____

5 you / know / your best friend
   _____

6 you / like / your favourite singer
   _____

4 Answer the survey questions in Activity 3. Use *since* or *for*.

1 (for) *I've lived in this town for ...*
2 (since) _____
3 (for) _____
4 (since) _____
5 (for) _____
6 (since) _____

5 Work with your partner. Ask the questions from Activity 3 and write their answers.

1 _____
2 _____
3 _____
4 _____
5 _____
6 _____

>> Grammar reference, page 124

Book Club ⑦

1 | After you read | **Read the diary on Pupil's Book page 92 again. Then number the places they visited in order. There are two places you don't need.**

 a

 b BOOKS

 c 1

 d THEATRE

 e

 f

 g

 h

2 **Read the sentences and circle *T* (true) or *F* (false). Explain your answers.**

1 The girl and her family arrived in New York at lunchtime. **T / F**
The girl and her family arrived in New York in the evening.

2 They visited the aquarium on the first morning of their trip. **T / F**
_____
_____

3 They went to the circus on Thursday evening. **T / F**
_____
_____

4 They visited the science museum before the art gallery. **T / F**
_____
_____

5 Macy's is the name of a world-famous theatre in New York. **T / F**
_____
_____

6 Mum and Dad didn't watch all of the show at the theatre. **T / F**
_____
_____

3 **Read the *Work with words* box. Then read the sentences and circle the correct options.**

Work with words
***-ed* and *-ing* adjectives** Some adjectives have two forms, ending with *-ed* and *-ing*. The *-ed* form describes how we feel. The *-ing* form describes a thing that makes us feel that way. *I was **tired** after all the sightseeing.* *I think sightseeing is **tiring**.*

1 Travelling long distances can be quite **tired / tiring**.

2 We were **amazed / amazing** by the circus performers.

3 My sister thinks art galleries are **interested / interesting**.

4 I'm not very **excited / exciting** about our trip to London.

5 I felt **embarrassed / embarrassing** when I fell down.

6 We thought the theatre show was **bored / boring**.

4 **Write two sentences with *-ed* adjectives and two sentences with *-ing* adjectives. Then compare with your partner.**

I think the Star Wars films are amazing!

1 **Read and complete the puzzle. What's the mystery word?**

```
6
1 P L A N E T A R I U M
              7
2 [         ]     [     ]
        5
3 [   ]   [     ]     
          4 [     ]   [     ]
```

1 → You can learn about the planets here.
2 → You can hear a band playing here.
3 → You can watch an exciting film here.
4 → You can see funny clowns here.
5 ↓ You can have fun ice skating here.
6 ↓ You can look at paintings here.
7 ↓ You can see fish here.

The mystery word is _____.

2 🎧 7.12 **Listen and choose the correct places.**

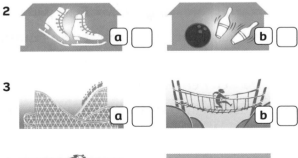

Present continuous for future arrangements

3 **Read and complete the sentences with the correct form of the Present continuous.**

1 My friends and I ___*aren't going*___ (not/go) to the safari park tomorrow.

2 I _____ (stay) with my grandparents next summer.

3 Harry _____ (not/go) bowling with his friends this evening.

4 You and your friends _____ (watch) a film this Saturday.

5 Megan _____ (visit) New York with her family next month.

6 My parents _____ (not/skate) tomorrow.

4 **Look at the notes and write about the children's plans for next Saturday. Use the Present continuous.**

Ben		Sue and Tom	
1 help dad – home	✓	4 go to planetarium	✓
2 have pizza – lunch	✗	5 eat lunch – café	✓
3 visit grandad	✓	6 watch film	✗

1 Ben *is helping his dad at home.*

2 Sue and Tom_____

3 _____

4 _____

5 _____

6 _____

5 💡 **Write five sentences about your plans for next Saturday using the Present continuous. Use the words in the box or your own ideas.**

> go shopping   have a party   help my parents
> play hockey   see friends   visit a castle
> watch cartoons   do the gardening   tidy my room

>> Grammar reference, page 124

1 **After you read** Read the text on Pupil's Book page 94 again. Tick (✓) the correct performance.

	Kagura	Cirque du Soleil
1 The performers act out traditional stories.	✓	
2 They perform the show all around the world.		
3 The performers wear expensive costumes during the show.		
4 The performers do acrobatics and juggling.		
5 You can watch the performance in Las Vegas.		
6 People can try on the performers' costumes.		

2 Answer the questions. Use complete sentences.

1 Why do people enjoy watching performers on stage?

   Watching performers on stage can be exciting.

2 How long have Japanese people performed Kagura?

   _____

3 When was the first Cirque du Soleil performance?

   _____

4 Why do Cirque du Soleil performers do their own make-up?

   _____

3 (7.14) Listen to a report about Ancient Greek theatre. Complete.

Theatre in Ancient Greece

Theatre was quite [1] _____*popular*_____ in ancient Greece. Most towns had a theatre where people could see [2] _____. It was usually on the side of a [3] _____, so people could see the stage. The word 'theatre' comes from a [4] _____ word for 'seeing place'. The Greeks watched two kinds of plays: [5] _____ stories called comedies and [6] _____ stories called tragedies. The actors wore [7] _____ and there was a group of [8] _____, called a chorus. Many of those Ancient Greek plays are popular today.

4 🌐 Work in groups. Choose one of the ancient Greek theatres in the box and find answers to the questions. Write a report about your theatre.

theatre of Dionysus   theatre of Epidaurus   theatre of Delphi   theatre of Dodona

1 Where is the theatre located?
2 How long ago did people build the theatre?
3 How many people could fit in the theatre?
4 What happened to the theatre?
5 What other information can you find about the theatre?

English in action
Buying tickets

1 Read the dialogue on Pupil's Book page 95 again. Who says these sentences? Write *C* (Customer) or *T* (Ticket seller).

1 [C] I don't know. How much is it?
2 [ ] Here are your tickets. Enjoy the play!
3 [ ] Can I have five tickets, please?
4 [ ] OK. That's forty-five pounds.
5 [ ] Hello, can I help you?
6 [ ] OK, then. Yes, please.

2 (7.17) Read and complete the dialogue. Then listen and check.

a Would you like to buy a programme?
b Alright. Here you are.
c Can I have two tickets, please?
d That's eighteen pounds in total.
e One adult and one child, please.
f Not much. It's only two pounds.

Man: Good morning. Can I help you?
Girl: Yes. ¹ *c Can I have two tickets, please?*
Man: Adults or children?
Girl: ² _____
Man: OK. That's sixteen pounds, please.
³ _____
Girl: I'm not sure. How much is it?
Man: ⁴ _____
Girl: OK, then. I'll take one programme.
Man: Great. ⁵ _____
Girl: ⁶ _____
Man: Thanks. And here are your tickets.

3 Work in pairs. Write a new dialogue. Use the dialogue in Activity 2 and the questions below to help you. Then act out the dialogue.

1 How many tickets do you need?

2 How much do the tickets cost?

3 How much does the programme cost?

4 What's the total amount you need to pay?

Pronunciation

4 (7.18) Listen and match. Then listen and repeat. Notice the coloured word endings. Then practise saying the questions and answers with your partner.

1 Have you ever wanted to be a writer?
2 This performer is rather boring.
3 Is your brother going to be an actor?
4 Do you want to order anything?

a No, he isn't. He wants to be a film director.
b I'd like another glass of water, please.
c No, never. I want to be a doctor!
d No, she isn't! She's great! That's my sister!

Words in context

1 Unscramble the words. Then label the pictures.

ezam
srahens
pzi ewri
ltuenn
elntamrpio
bcglniim ramfe

 1

 2

 3

maze _____ _____

 4

 5

 6

_____ _____ _____

2 Read the advert on Pupil's Book page 96 again. Complete with the correct imperatives.

1 ___Go___ along the paths and through the tunnels!

2 _____ and swing from tree to tree!

3 _____ fun on our high ropes or low ropes.

4 _____ our website or phone 0181 496 077.

5 _____ on our exciting zip wires high above the ground!

6 _____ on the high swing and touch the trees!

3 Answer the questions. Write complete sentences.

1 Where is the adventure playground located?

The adventure playground is located in Battington.

2 How long is the playground's climbing wall?

_____

3 What do people wear for the high activities?

_____

4 Where can children under the age of six have fun?

_____

5 Where can people have something to drink?

_____

4 Work in groups. Design your own adventure playground. Discuss the questions and make notes. Then share your ideas with the class.

1 What activities will your playground have?

2 What activities will there be for different ages?

3 What special equipment will people need?

4 What other areas will there be?

Literacy: adverts

Lesson 9

Writing

tip Writing
Use verbs (e.g. *ride, climb, jump, visit, watch*) and adjectives (e.g. *amazing, exciting, the most dangerous, the biggest*) to make your advert sound exciting!

1 **Read and complete the advert with the verbs and adjectives.**

enjoy   play   ride   ~~stay~~   beautiful   exciting   great   traditional

Kentwood Country Fair!
Farm fun for everyone!

Don't ¹ _stay_ at home this weekend!
Do something fun and ² _____ !
Come out and ³ _____ the **Kentwood Country Fair**.
It's a ⁴ _____ event that takes place every year.
You can see and ⁵ _____ with lots of farm animals.
The baby animals are ⁶ _____ and there are also big
animals like horses that you can ⁷ _____ .
It's a ⁸ _____ way to spend the day
and tickets are only £5!

Half price for children under 5!

2 **Plan an advert for a theme park.**

Include a logo. →
Use a slogan. →
Give important information using bullet points. →
Include a special offer. →
Make the design attractive. →

3 **Now write your advert.**

4 **Check your work. Tick (✓) the steps when you have done them.**

Have I included a good logo and slogan? ☐   Have I made the design look attractive? ☐
Have I used exciting verbs and adjectives? ☐   Have I included all the important information? ☐

1 Find and write ten job words.

1 *clown*   6 _____
2 _____   7 _____
3 _____   8 _____
4 _____   9 _____
5 _____   10 _____

C	I	T	K	A	S	E	R	O	E	D	L	E	R	C	R	P	E	R	E	D	R
L	R	E	S	T	E	N	C	B	M	I	L	T	E	O	E	E	M	C	M	E	E
O	W	R	E	E	R	T	A	A	O	A	A	D	C	M	S	R	R	O	U	S	N
W	N	I	C	R	P	E	R	T	C	N	B	A	N	P	O	F	O	S	T	I	G

2 Read and circle the correct places.

1 You can drive around and see lots of wild animals at a **safari park** / **planetarium**.
2 People can listen to their favourite singers in a **bookshop** / **concert hall**.
3 You can learn a lot about technology at a **circus** / **science museum**.
4 You can see lots of beautiful paintings in **an art gallery** / **a park**.
5 People can see lots of interesting fish in **an aquarium** / **a theatre**.

3 Write sentences with the Present perfect and *since* or *for*.

1 the boys / be / at school / two hours
The boys have been at school for two hours.
2 I / have / a phone / I was ten years old
3 Julie / live / in Madrid / six months
4 my grandparents / be / married / 1978
5 John / study / Spanish / four years
6 we / want / to go to bowling alley / last week

4 Write true sentences about your plans for the weekend.

1 see a horror film
I'm not seeing a horror film this weekend.
2 do my homework on Sunday
3 watch a football match
4 have pizza with friends
5 go shopping on Saturday
6 watch TV on Sunday

Self-evaluation

5 Answer the questions about your work in Unit 7.

1 How was your work in this unit? Choose. ☐ OK ☐ Good ☐ Excellent
2 Which lesson was your favourite? _____
3 Which parts of the unit were difficult for you? _____
4 What new things can you talk about now? _____
5 How can you work and learn better in the next unit? _____

Get ready for...

A2 Key for Schools Listening Part 3

 1 Read the task carefully. Make sure you know what you have to do.

 2 🎧 7.21 Listen and choose the sentence with a similar meaning.

1 **A** Omar has studied dance for ten years.
  B Omar became a ballet dancer when he was ten.
  C Omar has been a ballet dancer for ten years.

2 **A** Ava doesn't want to wear make-up.
  B Ava is going to put on some make-up.
  C Ava has never worn make-up.

 Exam
Before you begin, read and listen to the instructions to understand the context of the conversation.

Do! **3** 🎯 🎧 7.22 **Listen. For each question, choose the correct answer.**

1 You will hear a teacher talking to his students. What does he tell them to do?

  A Enjoy the trip to the art gallery.

  B Be polite and quiet during the tour.

  C Stay together with the group.

2 You will hear a girl, Betty, talking about jobs. What does Betty want to be?

  A a circus acrobat

  B a ballet teacher

  C a TV presenter

3 You will hear two boys making plans. Where are they going to go tomorrow?

  A the ice rink

  B the bowling alley

  C the 3D cinema

4 You will hear a girl buying tickets. How much is she going to spend?

  A ten pounds

  B eight pounds

  C five pounds

A2 Key for Schools Reading and Writing Part 4

 1 **Read the task carefully. Make sure you know what you have to do.**

 2 **Read and circle the correct words.**

1 Oliver's funny! He should be a **comic** / **comedian** / **comical** when he's older.

2 Where were you? I've been waiting here **for** / **before** / **since** half an hour!

3 Here are you tickets. Do you want **buy** / **buying** / **to buy** a programme?

 Exam

Work through all the questions, reading the whole sentence to make sure you circle the correct word to complete each gap.

Do! **3** 🎯 **For each question, choose and write the correct answer for each gap.**

My name's Michael and one of my favourite **(1)** _____places_____ in England is the National Space Centre, in Leicester. It's a science museum **(2)** _____ has six different galleries **(3)** _____. One of the galleries is a rocket tower that is 42 metres tall. The National Space Centre also has the UK's largest planetarium, which **(4)** _____ after a famous astronomer, Sir Patrick Moore. I enjoy **(5)** _____ to the planetarium to see shows because I want to be an astronomer one day. Lots of students visit the National Space Centre every year. Groups can also **(6)** _____ the night there and have a sleepover! My class did that two years ago, and we had an amazing time.

1 **A** place   **B** space   **C** places

2 **A** what   **B** that   **C** where

3 **A** to explore   **B** explore   **C** exploring

4 **A** named   **B** naming   **C** is named

5 **A** going   **B** to go   **C** be going

6 **A** have   **B** spend   **C** live

Awesome animals

Vocabulary

1 Complete the animal body parts. Then find and circle.

1 a _n_ t e _n_ _n_ _a_ e
2 b _ _ k
3 c _ a _ s
4 f _ _ s
5 f _ i _ _ e _ s
6 p _ _ s

7 p _ u _ h
8 s _ a _ _ _ s
9 s _ i _ _ s
10 t _ n _ _ e
11 w _ b _ _ d f _ _ t
12 w _ _ _ k _ _ s

S	Q	T	W	S	J	K	B	F	U
E	Q	O	E	R	A	W	E	L	S
N	T	N	B	E	H	N	E	I	C
I	M	G	B	K	E	B	A	P	A
P	H	U	E	S	J	Y	N	P	L
S	C	E	D	I	C	L	T	E	E
P	U	C	F	H	M	T	E	R	S
A	O	G	E	W	O	P	N	S	D
W	P	C	E	G	F	I	N	S	U
S	T	B	T	K	S	W	A	L	C
A	S	O	S	E	A	O	E	E	I

2 Read and complete the sentences with words from Activity 1.

1 Ants have ___antennae___ that they use to communicate.

2 A mother kangaroo carries its baby in a _____.

3 Seals use their _____ to move around.

4 A chameleon catches insects with its _____.

5 Sea urchins have long _____ for protection.

6 A snake has _____ all over its body.

3 💡 Read the *I'm learning* box. Then complete the table. Use a dictionary to help you.

bears   crocodiles   ducks   eagles   porcupines   lizards   rabbits   sharks   cats

I'm learning

Classifying animals
You can classify animals into groups by their body coverings.

*Dogs have **fur**.*
*Parrots have **feathers**.*
*Fish have **scales**.*
*Hedgehogs have **spines**.*

fur	feathers	scales	spines
Bears have fur.			

4 💡 Write three or more sentences about the body coverings of other animals you know.

1 (8.4) **Listen and complete the sentences from the dialogue on Pupil's Book page 102. Who says them? Write. Then listen and check.**

1 _Bobby_ There are lots of __different__ animals here.

2 _____ Hey! There's _____ over there!

3 _____ It might be a bear with long _____!

4 _____ It can't be a bird. It doesn't have _____.

5 _____ It doesn't have _____. Oh! It has spines!

6 _____ No, you shouldn't _____ it. It may be scared.

2 **Read the dialogue again and circle T (true) or F (false). Explain your answers.**

1 Bobby doesn't like the place
   where they are.   T / **F**

   Bobby says that he loves the place.

2 Arlo says he has already seen
   some frogs.   T / F

   _____

3 There aren't any bears where
   the team are.   T / F

   _____

4 The animal could be a bird
   because it has wings.   T / F

   _____

5 Lara says the animal doesn't
   have spines.   T / F

   _____

6 The team shouldn't pick up
   the hedgehog.   T / F

   _____

3 (8.5) **Read and complete the dialogues with the correct expressions. Then listen and check.**

(Watch out!) × 2   (Duh!) × 2   (It's so cute!) × 2

1 **A:** We're going to be late for school!
   B: No, we aren't. It's Saturday. _Duh!_

2 **A:** Look what we got last weekend!
   B: A puppy! _____

3 **A:** What's this? Are you cooking something?
   B: _____ It's very hot!

4 **A:** Come on! Let's cross the road.
   B: _____ There's a car!

5 **A:** What type of fish is a dolphin?
   B: Dolphins aren't fish.
   _____ They're mammals.

6 **A:** This is my pet guinea pig.
   B: _____ I want one, too!

4 **Work in pairs. Write another dialogue for each expression. Then act out the dialogues.**

may, might, could, can't, must

1 🎧 (8.8) **Listen and circle the correct sentences.**

1 a It may be a person. *(circled)*

   b It can't be a cat.

2 a It must be a type of fish.

   b It could be a dolphin.

3 a It could be a large rabbit.

   b It must be the neighour's dog.

4 a It can't be a bee.

   b It may be dangerous.

5 a It could be a sheep.

   b It might be a wild goat.

2 **Look and write sentences.**

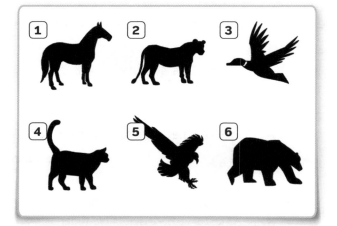

1 may / horse   *It may be a horse.*

2 could / lion   _____

3 must / duck   _____

4 can't / dog   _____

5 might / eagle   _____

6 may / polar bear   _____

3 **Read the riddles. Then guess the answers. Use each word in the box once.**

> can't   could ~~may~~ might must

1 It has four short legs and a long tail. It has scales on its body.
(crocodile)   *It may be a crocodile.*

2 It's a very big, dangerous cat. Its fur has black and orange stripes.
(tiger) _____

3 It's a black and white animal. It has four legs and it lives in Africa.
(penguin) _____

4 It's a very large animal that lives on land and in the water. It has four legs and a tail.
(hippo) _____

5 It's a large animal with four legs and lots of brown fur. It lives in the forest.
(bear) _____

4 💡 **Write riddles about three animals in the box. Write the answers with *may*, *might*, *could*, *can't* or *must*.**

> koala elephant giraffe monkey
> mouse ~~parrot~~ snake tortoise zebra
> chicken donkey alligator bat rhino

| It has wings and it lives in the jungle. | It could be a parrot. |

5 💬 **Work with your partner. Read the riddles from Activity 4 and write their guesses in your notebook.**

>> Grammar reference, page 125

WOW! Book Club 8

1 **After you read** Read the folk tale on Pupil's Book page 104 again. Then number the sentences in order.

- [ ] **a** The fish asked the platypus to join them.
- [ ] **b** The lions thought they were the best group.
- [ ] **c** The platypus said that all animals were important in different ways.
- [1] **d** All of the animals thought they were the most important.
- [ ] **e** The platypus decided not to join any group.
- [ ] **f** The lions invited the platypus to join them.
- [ ] **g** The birds wanted the platypus to join them.

2 Answer the questions about the folktale. Write complete sentences.

1 Why were the animals fighting about?
They were fighting about who was the best group of animals on Earth.

2 How are the lions and the platypus similar?

3 Why did the fish want the platypus to join them?

4 How is the platypus different from the fish?

5 How are the birds and the platypus similar?

6 What will happen if the platypus joins a group?

3 Read the *Work with words* box. Write the verbs with *-er* suffix. Then complete the sentences.

Work with words

verb + -er suffix

We can add *-er* to some verbs to make a new word for someone/something that does that action. For some verbs that end with a vowel and a consonant, we double the consonant before we add *-er*. For verbs that end in an e, we just add *-r*.

*present → present**er***
*run → run**ner***

farm	→	*farmer*
dive	→	_____
listen	→	_____
skate	→	_____
play	→	_____
read	→	_____

1 My uncle lives in the country and has lots of animals. He's a ___*farmer*___ .

2 A platypus can swim very quickly. It's also an excellent _____ .

3 I talk to my friend Laura about my problems. She's a good _____ .

4 Sam goes to the ice rink every Saturday. He's an excellent _____ .

5 Cristiano Ronaldo may be the world's most famous football _____ .

6 I borrow lots of books from the library because I'm a keen _____ .

4 Write sentences with the *-er* form of the verbs in the box. Then compare with your partner.

clean   dance   sing   teach   write

My dad loves sweeping the floor. He's a good cleaner.

Vocabulary and Grammar

1 **Read and circle the correct options.**

1 Sea turtles lay their eggs on sandy beaches. They (**dig**) / **hide** / **roar** holes in the sand

2 I have two dogs. They usually play nicely, but sometimes they **hide** / **dive** / **fight**.

3 My brother is frightened of bees and other insects that could **sting** / **die** / **fight** him.

4 We saw some lions at the zoo. They're really loud when they **run** / **dig** / **roar**.

5 I have two cats. They like to **bite** / **sting** / **hide** under my bed.

6 Some whales can **dig** / **dive** / **curl** more than 2,000 metres under the water.

2 (8.12) **Listen to a presentation about pill bugs. Then complete the sentences.**

Pill bugs

1 Pill bugs live on land, but only in ___wet places___ . They will _____ if they get too dry.

2 Pill bugs _____ and then carry them around in a tiny _____.

3 When there is danger, pill bugs can't _____ because they don't have _____.

4 Pill bugs can _____ from danger and they can also _____ into a ball.

5 Pill bugs aren't _____ to people because they can't _____ or _____.

First conditional: *if ..., ... will ...*

3 **Read and complete the sentences. Use the first conditional.**

1 If a lizard loses its tail in a fight, it ___will grow___ (grow) a new one.

2 If you _____ (not/be) nice to me, I will get angry with you.

3 If Kevin feels tired on Saturday, he _____ (not/play) football.

4 If Emma _____ (ask) her parents for a new tablet, they will buy one for her.

5 If my friends and I go scooting today, we _____ (have) fun.

6 If you _____ (not/do) your homework, you will fail the exam.

4 💡 **Read and complete the sentences with your own ideas. Use the first conditional.**

1 If I don't eat breakfast, ___I will feel hungry at school___ .

2 If my best friend forgets my birthday this year, _____.

3 If you don't water the plants in your garden, _____.

4 If you help me study for the English test, _____.

5 If the weather isn't very nice this weekend, _____.

6 If I visit London with my family this year, _____.

5 💬 **Compare your responses in Activity 4 with your partner. Who wrote the best response?**

≫ Grammar reference, page 125

 **Culture** ⑧

1 **After you read** Read the text on Pupil's Book page 106 again. What do these sentences describe?

1 It has a large bird on its national flag. *Ecuador*

2 They use noises and smells to communicate. _____

3 Its national animal is a very large lizard. _____

4 They don't build nests for their eggs. _____

5 Its national animal is the ring-tailed lemur. _____

6 They use their tongues to locate animals. _____

2 Read the sentences and circle *T* (true) or *F* (false). Explain your answers.

1 A lemur's tail is easy to see in the forest. (T)/ F
Its tail is easy to see because it's striped.

2 Lemurs are good climbers, but they aren't good runners. T / F
_____

3 Condors are quite small birds that eat dead animals. T / F
_____

4 Condors have big wings that help them fly easily. T / F
_____

5 Komodo dragons are very dangerous to other animals. T / F
_____

6 It's easy for people to run away from komodo dragons. T / F
_____

3 (8.14) Listen to a report about another unusual animal. Complete.

The kiwi

The kiwi is the national animal of ¹_____ *New Zealand* _____. It's an unusual bird because it can't ²_____. Kiwis are about the size of a ³_____, so they are quite small but their eggs are very big for their size. Kiwis have small, brown ⁴_____ and a long, thin ⁵_____, which they use to catch ⁶_____. Kiwis live in ⁷_____ and hunt at night. Kiwis are in danger because people brought other ⁸_____ to New Zealand, such as ⁹_____ and rats. These animals are killing kiwis and stealing their ¹⁰_____.

4 Work in groups. Choose one of the national animals in the box and find answers to the questions. Write a report about your national animal.

> brown bear (Finland)   gyrfalcon (Iceland)   pharaoh hound (Malta)
> red kangaroo (Australia)   vicuña (Peru)   bald eagle (USA)

1 Where does the animal live?
2 What does the animal look like?
3 What can/can't the animal do?
4 What is special or unusual about it?
5 Is the animal in danger now? Why?

English in action
Saying what you like and don't like

1 (8.17) **Read and complete the dialogue. Then listen and check.**

> **a** They're clean and very quiet.
> **b** I'm not keen on cats.
> **c** All kinds! But my favourites are parrots.
> **d** ~~Yes, I do! I'm crazy about them!~~
> **e** Well, I find birds very interesting.
> **f** I don't mind them. And you?

Boy: Do you like cats?
Girl: ¹ _d Yes, I do! I'm crazy about them!_   What about you?
Boy: ² _____ I don't like their fur. I really don't like them at all.
Girl: Do you like lizards?
Boy: ³ _____
Girl: I quite like lizards. ⁴_____ What animals do you like?
Boy: ⁵_____ I enjoy watching them.
Girl: Me, too. What kinds of birds do you like?
Boy: ⁶_____
Girl: Oh, I can't stand parrots. They talk too much.

2 **Read and complete the sentences with your own ideas about animals.**

1 I'm crazy about _____ _dogs_ _____ .
2 I find _____ really interesting.
3 I quite like_____ .
4 I don't mind_____ .

5 I'm not keen on _____ .
6 I don't like _____ at all.
7 I can't stand _____ .

3 **Work in pairs. Compare your ideas from Activity 2.**

Pronunciation

4 (8.18) **Read and listen to the words. Circle the stressed parts. Then practise saying the words with your partner.**

1 a (qui)et (don)key
2 a dangerous tiger
3 an unusual jellyfish

4 a difficult problem
5 an exciting holiday
6 a horrible idea

7 an interesting story
8 a funny giraffe
9 an unfriendly gorilla

Words in context

1 **Read and complete the definitions.**

~~vertebrate~~   amphibian   invertebrate   insect   reptile   mammal

1 A _____vertebrate_____ is an animal that has a backbone.

2 An _____ is an animal that lives in water and on land.

3 A _____ is an animal that gives birth to its babies and the babies drink their mother's milk.

4 An _____ is an animal that doesn't have a backbone.

5 A _____ has hard scales all over its body and it lays eggs.

6 An _____ is an invertebrate that has six legs.

2 **Read the fact files on Pupil's Book page 108 again. Complete.**

1 The Golden mantella frog is a brightly-coloured ____amphibian____ that lives in the forests of Madagascar. It's very small, but it's also _____, so other animals don't eat it.

2 The Mata mata turtle is found in many _____ ponds and rivers in South America. This reptile can _____ about 15 kilogrammes and be up to 45 centimetres long.

3 The Giant prickly stick insect lives in the forests of _____. This unusual invertebrate is quite long – about 20 centimetres – and it has very long _____.

4 The Western long-beaked echidna is a strange _____ because it has a beak and it lays _____, like a bird. It's found in the mountains and forests of New Guinea.

3 **Answer the questions. Write complete sentences.**

1 How long can a Golden mantella frog be?

  It can be two to three centimetres long.

2 Why do Golden mantella frogs have a bright colour?

  _____

3 What things does the Mata mata turtle eat?

  _____

4 Why does a Mata mata turtle need such a long nose?

  _____

5 Why is it hard to see a Giant prickly stick insect?

  _____

6 How much do Western long-beaked echidnas usually weigh?

  _____

4 **Work in groups. Choose an animal you know about. Discuss the questions and make notes. Then share your ideas with the class.**

1 What type of animal is it?
2 Where does it live?
3 What does it look like?

4 What does it eat?
5 is there anything unusual about it?

Literacy: fact files

Writing

> **Remember to use** *its* **and** *it's* **correctly:**
> *it's* means *it is* or *it has*
> *its* is for possession
> **It's (It is)** *better at climbing than jumping!*
> *It uses* **its** *very long nose* **(possession)** *to breathe.*

1 **Read and complete the sentences with** *it's* **and** *its.*

1 An echidna can swim well. It uses _____*its*_____ long nose to breathe in the water.

2 Ring-tailed lemurs have a long tail. _____ used to fight and to communicate.

3 A condor is a very large bird. _____ open wings can be 3 metres across.

4 A komodo dragon uses _____ tongue to taste the air and find food.

5 A lizard is a type of reptile. _____ in the same family as the crocodile.

6 A giraffe eats leaves from tall trees. That's why _____ neck is so long.

2 Plan a fact file about an unusual wild animal.

Look at books or the internet to find facts to include. →	_____
Use headings and put colons (:) after them. →	_____
Don't write in full sentences. Use simple notes. →	_____
Use abbreviations for size and weight: *m* (metres), *cm* (centimetres), *kg* (kilogrammes), etc. →	_____
Include some special and unusual facts. →	_____

3 **Now write your fact file.**

4 **Check your work. Tick (✓) the steps when you have done them.**

Have I included some interesting and unusual facts? ☐

Have I listed my facts in note form? ☐

Have I used abbreviations correctly? ☐

Have I used *it's* and *its* correctly? ☐

1 **Label the parts of the animals.**

1	2	3	4	5	6

beak   _____   _____   _____   _____   _____

2 **Read and complete the sentences with the correct form of the verbs in the box.**

> dig   fight   fly away   hide   ~~roar~~   sting

1 Lions make a lot of noise when they _roar_ .

2 Our cat often _____ behind the sofa.

3 You and I argue, but we don't _____ .

4 My dog _____ holes in the garden.

5 Some insects can _____ you.

6 If a bird is scared, it will _____ .

3 **Guess the animals. Use the words in the box and _may_, _might_, _could_, _can't_ or _must_ in that order.**

> eagle   elephant   giraffe   lion   monkey   mouse   parrot   ~~snake~~   tortoise   zebra

1 It's long and it doesn't have legs.   _It may be a snake._ _____

2 It's very big and grey. It has big ears.   _____

3 It has long legs, a tail and lots of hair.   _____

4 It has two legs and it lays eggs.   _____

5 It's black and white and it looks like a horse.   _____

4 **Read and complete the first conditional sentences so that they are true for you.**

1 If I pass my English exam, _I will be very happy._ _____

2 If you call me after 11 o'clock at night, _____

3 If I get some money for my birthday, _____

4 If students don't do their homework, _____

5 If I stay up really late tonight, _____

Self-evaluation

5 **Answer the questions about your work in Unit 8.**

1 How was your work in this unit? Choose.   ☐ OK   ☐ Good   ☐ Excellent

2 Which lesson was your favourite? _____

3 Which parts of the unit were difficult for you? _____

4 What new things can you talk about now? _____

5 How can you work and learn better in the next unit? _____

A2 Key for Schools Listening Part 3

 1 Read the task carefully. Make sure you know what you have to do.

 2 (8.20) Listen and choose. Which animal will George write about? Then explain your answer.

A zebra

B tiger

C eagle

Do! **3** 🎯 (8.21) **For each question, choose the correct answer. You will hear Emma talking to David about science projects. Which animal will each person write about?**

> **tip Exam**
>
> Read the words in the list carefully first and note that they are all from the same lexical set.

1 Laura ☐

2 David ☐

3 Emma ☐

4 Bryan ☐

5 Lucy ☐

A jellyfish

B cheetah

C condor

D hedgehog

E crocodile

F dolphin

G lemur

H platypus

A2 Key for Schools Reading and Writing Part 5

Think! **1** Read the task carefully. Make sure you know what you have to do.

Try! **2** Complete the sentences with ONE word.

1 Look at how fast that dog is eating! It _____ be very hungry.

2 I'm sorry, but I _____ talk now. I'm doing my history project.

3 Please be quiet. If you're noisy, the birds _____ fly away.

Do! **3** 🎯 For each question, write the correct answer in each gap. Write ONE word for each gap.

tip Exam

Once all the gaps are completed, read the whole text again to make sure it makes sense.

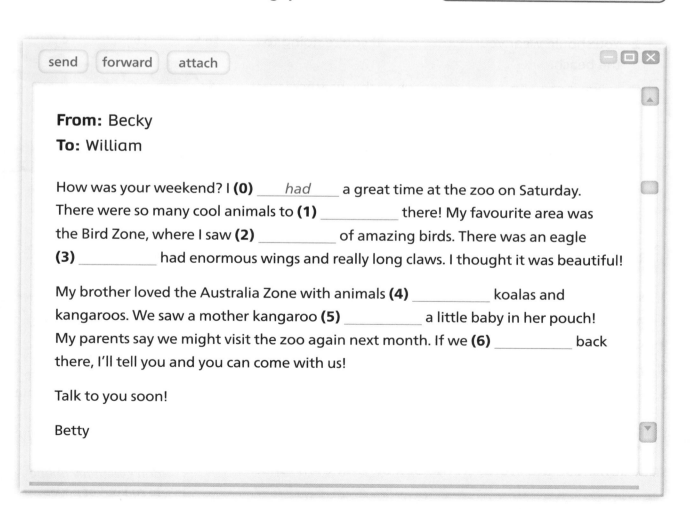

send | forward | attach

From: Becky
To: William

How was your weekend? I **(0)** _____had_____ a great time at the zoo on Saturday. There were so many cool animals to **(1)** _____ there! My favourite area was the Bird Zone, where I saw **(2)** _____ of amazing birds. There was an eagle **(3)** _____ had enormous wings and really long claws. I thought it was beautiful!

My brother loved the Australia Zone with animals **(4)** _____ koalas and kangaroos. We saw a mother kangaroo **(5)** _____ a little baby in her pouch! My parents say we might visit the zoo again next month. If we **(6)** _____ back there, I'll tell you and you can come with us!

Talk to you soon!

Betty

Travel

Vocabulary

1 **Read and complete the definitions.**

1 _____Soap_____ is something you use to wash your body in the shower.

2 A _____ makes sleeping on a plane more comfortable.

3 A _____ has your photo in it. You carry it for identification.

4 You wear a _____ to stay dry when the weather is wet.

5 A _____ carries all your clothes when you go on holiday.

6 You use a _____ to clean your teeth every day.

2 **Read and complete the sentences with words from Activity 1.**

[d] **1** I'll need a ___charger___ for my phone and for my tablet.

[ ] **2** You should wear your _____ if you're going to the beach.

[ ] **3** I always carry an _____ when the weather is wet.

[ ] **4** We'll need to take some _____ if we feel sick during the trip.

[ ] **5** You should read a _____ so you know what to do when you arrive on holiday.

[ ] **6** I always carry my shampoo and soap in my _____.

a   b   c

d   e   f

3 **Read the *I'm learning* box. Then write sentences describing everyday situations.**

1 (suitcase) *I have a red suitcase that I always take with me on holiday.*

2 (pillow) _____

3 (soap) _____

4 (passport) _____

5 (raincoat) _____

> **I'm learning**
>
> **Describing everyday situations**
> You can learn new words better if you use them in sentences about everyday situations.
>
> (charger) *I always carry my charger because I don't want my phone to run out of power.*
> (flip-flops) *I usually wear flip-flops at the swimming pool.*

4 **Write three or more sentences about everyday situations. Use the words in the box or your own ideas.**

> laptop   earphones   toothbrush   trainers
> TV   guidebook   plaster   sunglasses

1 (9.4) **Listen to the dialogue on Pupil's Book page 114 again. Then read and complete the sentences.**

1 Lara asks Ting if she's _____ready_____ for their trip to Madrid.

2 Ting says she's going to take a small _____.

3 Lara is going to put her raincoat into her _____.

4 Ting tells Lara that she doesn't have an _____.

5 Lara says they can share her _____, soap and shampoo.

6 Ting is going to look for her _____ at home.

2 **Read the sentences and circle T (true) or F (false). Explain your answers.**

1 Lara isn't going to take a camera on the trip.   T / **F**

She's going to take a rucksack with her _____
camera in it. _____

2 Ting is going to take sweatshirts and jeans.   T / F

_____

3 Lara doesn't think they will need an umbrella.   T / F

_____

4 Ting tells Lara that she should bring her passport.   T / F

_____

5 Ting knows they are going to visit Madrid.   T / F

_____

6 Lara is going to buy a guidebook at a bookshop.   T / F

_____

3 (9.5) **Read and complete the dialogues with the correct expressions. Then listen and check.**

Of course! x 2   Good plan! x 2   Thanks for your help. x 2

1 **A:** I want to have a party next weekend. Can you help me?

B: ¹ _____Of course!_____ You know I love parties.

A: I'm going to have the party in our garden, so I can invite lots of people.

B: ² _____ I can bring some music and I can help you prepare the food.

A: That's fantastic! ³ _____

B: Oh, it's no problem!

2 **A:** We've done it! The house is finally tidy!

B: Yes, it is. ⁴ _____

A: You're welcome.

B: I'm hungry. Can you help me make some pizza?

A: ⁵ _____ Pizza's my favourite food!

B: Great. Then after lunch we could go to the 3D cinema.

A: ⁶ _____ There's a new science-fiction film that I really want to watch.

4 **Work in pairs. Write another dialogue for each expression. Then act out the dialogues.**

going to and *will*

1 (9.8) **Listen and tick (✓) the correct pictures.**

1 Where is the girl going to go for the holidays?

2 What will the weather be like in France?

3 How is her family going to travel?

4 What will the girl send the boy?

2 **Read and circle the correct options.**

Sonia: What (are you going to) / will you do next weekend?

Ted: If it's hot and sunny, **I'll / I'm going to** go camping.

Sonia: Can I come, too?

Ted: Of course! If you come, will you bring your camping stove and a sleeping mat? **I'm going to / I'll** take a tent.

Sonia: OK, **I'm going to / I will**. Anything else?

Ted: I think **we'll / we're going to** go hiking, too, so **I'm going to / we'll** take my compass. Can you bring a first-aid kit?

Sonia: No problem. Where **are we going to / will we** go camping?

Ted: **We'll / We're going to** go camping in the forest. It's really great there.

Sonia: That sounds fun!

3 **Read and complete the sentences with the correct form of *going to* or *will*.**

1 I'm hungry. I think I ___will make___ (make) a sandwich.

2 We _____ (go) to the cinema later. We bought our tickets online.

3 Emma _____ (play) basketball today. She has her piano lesson at 4 o'clock.

4 Don't worry about your journey to London next week. You _____ (have) any problems.

5 If you wait a minute, I _____ (help) you with those big suitcases.

6 My friends _____ (watch) videos today. They want to go cycling because it's a sunny day.

4 💬 **Read and complete the sentences with your own ideas. Then compare your answers with your partner.**

1 If you call me this evening, I _____

2 On Saturday afternoon, I _____

3 If you want to go skiing, I _____

4 Next summer, my family _____

5 This weekend, I _____

6 I found some money in the street, I think I _____

>>> Grammar reference, page 126

 **Book Club** **9**

1 After you read ⟩ **Read the science-fiction story on Pupil's Book page 116 again. Who says these lines? Complete and write.**

1 ___Dex___ There's ___nothing___ to do in the holidays.

2 _____ We're going to go on an exciting journey _____.

3 _____ Are we nearly there _____?

4 _____ Wake up Dex! We _____ in fifteen minutes.

5 _____ Well, not really, but there's a Moon _____ at three o'clock.

6 _____ When do we go _____ to Earth?

2 **Answer the questions. Write complete sentences.**

1 What did Dex want at the beginning of the story?   *He wanted to do something exciting in the holidays.*

2 How did Dex, Molly and Mum get to the launch pad? _____

3 Why did Dex and Molly need pillows for the flight? _____

4 How could Dex see Mars from their hotel room? _____

5 Why didn't Dex and Molly like the hotel very much? _____

6 Where does Dex want to go when he gets home? _____

3 **Read the *Work with words* box. Then look and write phrasal verbs with *on* or *off*.**

turn   put   ~~get~~   take   turn   get

Work with words

Phrasal verbs with *on* and *off*

There are many phrasal verbs with the prepositions *on* and *off*.

get + *on* = ***get on*** / *take* + *off* = ***take off***

1 ___get on___   2 _____

3 _____   4 _____   5 _____   6 _____

4 💡 **Write sentences using the six phrasal verbs from Activity 3.**

1 (9.12) **Listen and complete the notes.**

Journey to Buenos Aires: Saturday

1 _Leave_ home: _6.00_
2 _____ the plane: _____
3 Plane will _____: _____
4 _____ in Buenos Aires: _____
5 _____ the plane: _____
6 _____ the centre of town then have lunch: _____

2 **Look, read and complete the sentences.**

1 They're going to
   go on a journey .

2 He's going to
   _____ .

3 They want to
   _____ .

4 'Amy, please
   _____!'

5 The plane's going to _____ very soon.

6 'Excuse me. Please _____.'

Present simple for the future

3 **Imagine you're going on a school trip to a museum. Complete the sentences with the Present simple for the future.**

arrive   go   get on   finish   have
meet   explore   leave   start

1 Everyone _____gets on_____ the bus at 8.45 in the morning.
2 The bus _____ school at 9.00.
3 The bus _____ at the museum at 9.30.
4 We _____ our tour guide at 9.45.
5 The museum tour _____ at 10.00.
6 The museum tour _____ at 12.15.
7 We _____ lunch in the café at 12.30.
8 We _____ the gardens after lunch.
9 The bus _____ back to school at 3.00.

4 **Look at the travel notes and write about a school trip to the circus. Use the Present simple for the future.**

School trip to circus

- Bus (leave school): 12.00
- Bus (arrive at circus): 12.45
- Have lunch: 1.00
- Take seats in circus tent: 1.45
- Circus (start): 2.00
- Circus (finish): 4.00
- Everyone gets on bus: 4.15
- Bus (leave circus): 4.30
- Bus (arrive at school): 5.15

The bus leaves school at 12.00.
_____
_____
_____
_____

>> Grammar reference, page 126

1 **After you read** Read the text on Pupil's Book page 118 again. Tick (✓) the correct railway.

	Settle to Carlisle	Trans-Siberian
1 It's the longest railway in the world.	✓	
2 The people on the train go from Europe to Asia.		
3 The train travels through fourteen tunnels.		
4 You start in England and finish in Scotland.		
5 It travels next to the biggest lake in the world.		
6 You travel during the night on this train.		

2 Read the sentences and circle *T* (true) or *F* (false). Explain your answers.

1 The railway from Settle to Carlisle is 140 kilometres long.   **T / (F)**
The railway from Settle to Carlisle
is 115 kilometres long.

2 The trains that go from Settle to Carlisle are very modern.   **T / F**
_____

3 If you want to explore, you can leave the Settle to Carlisle train.   **T / F**
_____

4 The Trans-Siberian journey is longer than 9,000 kilometres.   **T / F**
_____

5 You can finish the Trans-Siberian journey in one day.   **T / F**
_____

6 Not many people take food on the Trans-Siberian train.   **T / F**

3 (9.14) Listen to an advert for another famous railway. Complete the text.

If going on ¹_____slow_____ but amazing train rides is what you like, you should buy a ²_____ for the Glacier Express. This ³_____ railway in Switzerland travels between Zermatt and St. Moritz. It takes about ⁴_____ hours to travel 290 kilometres through high ⁵_____, deep valleys and beautiful ⁶_____. The train goes through ⁷_____ and over hundreds of bridges. The ⁸_____ part of the journey is the Oberlap Pass, which is about 2,130 metres high. The train's very large ⁹_____ will let you enjoy a fantastic view. Don't forget your ¹⁰_____!

4 Work in groups. Choose one of the railways in the box and find answers to the questions. Write about your famous railway.

Black Sea Express (Bulgaria)   California Zephyr (USA)
Oslo to Bergen (Norway)   The Blue Train (South Africa)   The Ghan Train (Australia)

1 Where does the railway start and finish?
2 How far does the train travel?
3 How long does the journey take?

4 What can people see as they travel?
5 What is unusual about this railway?

English in action
Saying how you feel about the future

1 🎧(9.17) **Read and complete the dialogue. Then listen and check.**

a I'm really excited about it.
b I can't wait to go, because
c ~~I'm really looking forward to~~
d My family and I are going to
e I'm not looking forward to that part.
f worried about the language

Boy: ¹ _c I'm really looking forward to_ the summer break!

Girl: What are you going to do?

Boy: ² _____ to go windsurfing in Spain.

Girl: Wow! That sounds like fun.

Boy: Yes! ³ _____ I love windsurfing. But I'm also ⁴ _____. I don't speak Spanish!

Girl: Where in Spain are you going to go windsurfing?

Boy: At a beach in the south, near Tarifa.

Girl: That sounds great! I'm going to Norway with my parents and ⁵ _____

Boy: Really? How are you going to travel?

Girl: By plane, but ⁶ _____

Boy: Why is that? Are you afraid of flying?

Girl: Yes, a little, but I'll be fine.

2 💡 **Answer the questions with your own ideas. Explain your reasons.**

1 What are you excited about doing this week? Why?
This week I'm excited about ...
because ...

2 Is there something you can't wait to do next weekend?
_____
_____

3 What are you really looking forward to doing this school year?
_____
_____

4 Is there something you aren't looking forward to doing?
_____
_____

3 💬 **Work in pairs. Compare your ideas from Activity 2.**

5 Are you worried about anything at the moment?
_____

Pronunciation

4 💬🎧(9.18) **Read and listen to the questions. Circle the stressed parts. Then practise saying the questions with your partner.**

1 (Where) are you going to (go)?
2 When are you going to leave?
3 How are you going to travel?

4 Where are you going to stay?
5 What are you going to see?
6 Who are you going to meet?

5 💡 **Imagine you're going on a journey. Write answers to the questions in Activity 4.**

Reading

Words in context

1 Read and complete the sentences.

express   busy   lucky   ~~lovely~~   brand-new   wonderful

1 What a _____ lovely _____ photo of your family. Everyone looks so happy.
2 The hospital was very _____. I had to wait an hour to see the doctor.
3 My parents used to have an old car, but now they have a _____ one.
4 Robin won first prize at the science fair! That's _____ news!
5 Don't take the regular train. You'll be late. Take the _____ train.
6 The weather was sunny when I visited London in February. I was so _____!

2 Read the itinerary on Pupil's Book page 120 again. Then read and complete.

On Day 1, pupils must be at the airport before ¹_____ 1.15 pm _____ because the plane takes off at ²_____. The plane lands in London at ³_____ and then pupils go to the hotel. They won't have dinner until ⁴_____ in the evening. On Day 2, they will visit the Tower of London in the ⁵_____. Then they will have time for other things in the ⁶_____.

On Day 3, they won't go to the Tate Museum in the ⁷_____, because they do that in the ⁸_____. On the last day, their plane leaves at ⁹_____ in the morning. They arrive back at school at ¹⁰_____ in the afternoon.

3 Answer the questions. Write complete sentences.

1 How are the pupils going to get to the hotel?
   They are going to go on the underground.

2 What kind of shoes should they pack
   for the trip?

   _____

3 What are they going to do for lunch on
   Day 2?

   _____

4 Why are they going to bring their swimsuits?

   _____

5 Why will they enjoy going on the
   London Eye?

   _____

6 What time are they going to land at home?

   _____

4 Work in groups. Plan a one-day school trip. Choose one of the places in the box or a place you know. Discuss the questions and make notes. Then share your ideas with the class.

a theme park   a local farm   a planetarium   a science museum   a sports centre

1 Where will you go for your trip?
2 What time will you start and finish the trip?
3 How will you travel there and back?

4 What will you do and see there?
5 Where will you have lunch or a snack?
6 What will you probably enjoy the most?

Literacy: itineraries

Writing

1 Read and complete the instructions. Use the correct form of the words in the box.

> need (x 2)   bring (x 2)   must (x 2)   not/forget (x 2)

tip Writing

You can give instructions in different ways:
You must listen carefully to your teacher.
Don't forget your passport!
You need to bring a wallet.
Bring your sunhat.

1 ___Don't forget___ your umbrella. The weather could be rainy.

2 _____ a pillow so that you can sleep during the flight.

3 You _____ stay together. We don't want to lose you!

4 You _____ bring your passport with you.

5 _____ to add the flour to the cake mixture.

6 You _____ type in your password before you start.

7 _____ a sweatshirt. It might be cold.

8 You _____ turn off the lights when you leave a room.

2 Plan a four-day itinerary for a visitor to your town or city.

- Use headings to organise your work: *Day 1*, *Day 2*, etc.
- Divide days into morning and afternoon: *am* or *pm*.
- Include important times for planes, trains, buses, etc.
- Describe the activities simply and clearly.
- Give useful advice and suggestions about what to bring.

3 Now write your itinerary.

4 Check your work. Tick (✓) the steps when you have done them.

Have I organised my work clearly? ☐

Have I described the activities correctly? ☐

Have I included important information? ☐

Have I included useful advice and suggestions? ☐

1 Find and write nine words for travel items. Then match them to the pictures.

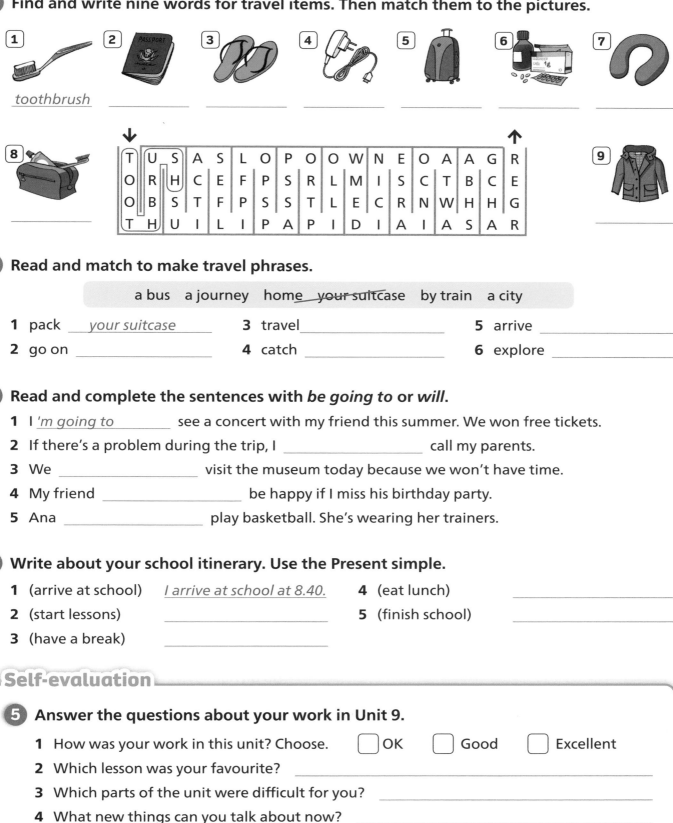

1 toothbrush **2** _____ **3** _____ **4** _____ **5** _____ **6** _____ **7** _____

8 _____ **9** _____

2 Read and match to make travel phrases.

a bus   a journey   home   ~~your suitcase~~   by train   a city

1 pack ___your suitcase___   **3** travel _____   **5** arrive _____

2 go on _____   **4** catch _____   **6** explore _____

3 Read and complete the sentences with *be going to* or *will*.

1 I *'m going to* _____ see a concert with my friend this summer. We won free tickets.

2 If there's a problem during the trip, I _____ call my parents.

3 We _____ visit the museum today because we won't have time.

4 My friend _____ be happy if I miss his birthday party.

5 Ana _____ play basketball. She's wearing her trainers.

4 Write about your school itinerary. Use the Present simple.

1 (arrive at school) *I arrive at school at 8.40.*   **4** (eat lunch) _____

2 (start lessons) _____   **5** (finish school) _____

3 (have a break) _____

Self-evaluation

5 Answer the questions about your work in Unit 9.

1 How was your work in this unit? Choose. ☐ OK ☐ Good ☐ Excellent

2 Which lesson was your favourite? _____

3 Which parts of the unit were difficult for you? _____

4 What new things can you talk about now? _____

5 How can you work and learn better next year? _____

Get ready for...

 1 Read the task carefully. Make sure you know what you have to do.

 2 (9.21) How many days will Sophia be in London? Listen and choose the correct picture. Then explain your answer.

A

B

C

Do! **3** 🎯 (9.22) Listen. For each question, choose the correct answer.

 tip Exam
Listen to the recording for the gist meaning and choose the best option.

1 What did David forget to put in his suitcase?

A ☐   B ☐   C ☐

3 Who is meeting Frank at the bus station?

A ☐   B ☐   C ☐

2 When is Sarah going to visit her aunt?

A ☐   B ☐   C ☐

4 Where are the man and woman going to go on holiday?

A ☐   B ☐   C ☐

A2 Key for Schools Reading and Writing Part 7

 1 Read the task carefully. Make sure you know what you have to do.

 2 Look at the picture. Answer the questions.

1 Where is the man?

_____

_____

2 What is he doing?

_____

_____

3 What can he see?

_____

_____

Do! **3** Look at the three pictures. Write the story shown in the pictures. Write 35 words or more.

tip **Exam**

Look at all three pictures first and think about how they could tell a story. Then plan a sentence for each picture.

_____

_____

_____

_____

_____

_____

Lara's Learning Club

Language booster 3

1 Write the months in order. Think about the seasons in your country and colour the months.

July   November   March   June   December   August   February
April   October   ~~January~~   May   September

spring = green   summer = yellow   autumn = red   winter = blue

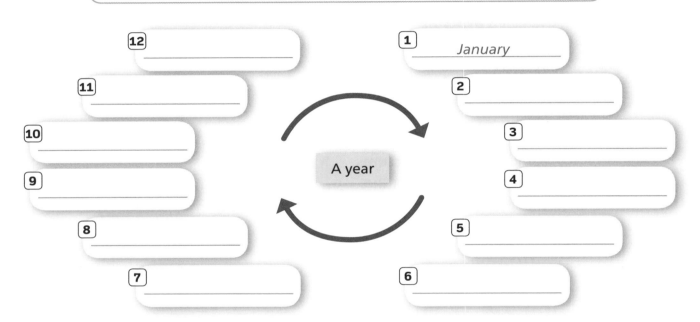

12 _____

11 _____

10 _____

9 _____

8 _____

7 _____

A year

1 _____January_____

2 _____

3 _____

4 _____

5 _____

6 _____

2 Complete the crossword. Find and write the hidden word.

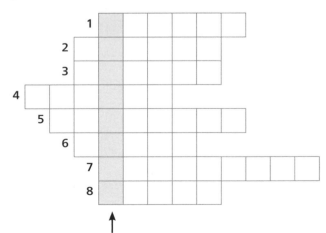

1 The season before the summer.
2 The season after the summer.
3 The opposite of midnight.
4 The coldest season.
5 The last month.
6 The third month.
7 The ninth month.
8 The opposite of late.

Something that people take on holiday: _____

3 Read the traditional rhyme and write the missing months.

12 ——— 5 — Calendar ——— 3 — 8

16

Thirty days have ¹S_____,
April, June and ²N_____.
All the rest have thirty-one,

Except for ³F_____ alone,
And that has twenty-eight days clear,
But twenty-nine in each leap year.

13

——— 26 ——— 7 ——————— 30 —

4 💡 Write the seasons in the table. Then write words you associate with each one.

Spring			
flowers	ice cream		

5 🎧 (LB3.3) Listen to the dialogue on Pupil's Book page 125 again. Answer the questions.

1 What time is it where Amy is? _____
2 What time is it where Rob Is? _____
3 What time does Dad want to call on Sunday? _____
4 What time does Amy ask him to call? _____
5 What's the time difference between the two countries? _____

6 Read and match.

1 Our flight leaves at quarter to five!
2 I'm playing tennis at 9 am tomorrow.
3 She always calls me on Sunday at four o'clock.
4 My birthday party starts at half past five in the afternoon.
5 They're catching the bus at quarter to eleven.
6 The planetarium closes at quarter past seven.

7 💡 Complete the sentences about you.

1 In the summer holidays, I get up at _____.
2 On school days, I go to bed at _____.
3 My birthday's in _____. It's in the _____.
4 The weather in my country is _____ in autumn.
5 I'm going to go to _____ in the summer.
6 When it's midday in my country, it's midnight in _____.

Grammar reference

1

Lesson 3: Present simple and Present continuous

1 **Read and complete.**

does   now   ~~play~~   doing   very often   wearing

Present simple		
I / You / We / They	¹_____play_____ badminton	after school.
	don't go scooting	² _____.
He / She	³ _____ gymnastics	twice a week.
	doesn't play hockey	on Mondays.

Present continuous		
I'm	(not) ⁴_____ jeans	today.
He's / She's	(not) doing athletics	⁵ _____.
You're / We're / They're	(not) ⁶_____ yoga	at the moment.

2 **Make sentences with the correct form of the Present simple or Present continuous.**

1 play / friends / not / now / play / volleyball / my

My friends are not playing
volleyball now.

2 cartoons / Diana / after / watch / often / school _____

3 cycling / we / week / a / go / twice / not _____

4 boots / wear / Tom / his / today / new _____

Lesson 5: State verbs

3 **Read and complete with examples.**

State verbs		
I / You / We / They	like / don't like	¹___doing the gardening___.
	love / hate	² _____.
He / She	prefers	⁴ _____.
Do you	know / believe	⁵ _____?

4 **Write sentences about people and their free-time activities. Use state verbs.**

1 winter sports   _I don't like skiing, but my brother loves it._

2 summer sports   _____

3 music   _____

4 TV shows   _____

5 hobbies   _____

Lesson 3: *could/couldn't, had to/didn't have to*

1 **Read and complete.**

can ~~can't~~ could doesn't have had don't have

Present simple		
I / You / We / They	can / [1] _____can't_____ have to / [2] _____ to	make a phone call. send a message.
He / She	[3] _____ / can't has to / [4] _____ to	search the internet. play the game.

Past simple		
I / You / He / She We / They	[5] _____ / couldn't	type in a password. go online.
	[6] _____ to / didn't have to	take a selfie.

2 **Read and complete the sentences with the correct form of *can* or *have to*.**

1 People _____couldn't_____ send emails in the 1950s because they didn't have computers.

2 We _____ buy lunch today. We brought some sandwiches from home.

3 My older brother _____ swim really fast. He wins lots of competitions.

4 My mum _____ get up early every day. She starts work at 8.00 am.

5 I _____ meet you at the café this afternoon. I have a piano lesson.

6 Adam _____ go home because he wasn't feeling very well.

Lesson 5: Comparative adverbs

3 **Read and complete with examples.**

Comparative adverbs			
adverbs ending in -*ly*		**short adverbs**	
carefully	more [1] _____carefully_____	hard	[6] _____
[2] _____	more clearly	[7] _____	faster
noisily	[3] _____	**irregular adverbs**	
[4] _____	more quickly	badly	[8] _____
quietly	[5] _____	[9] _____	better

4 **Write sentences to compare people. Use comparative adverbs.**

1 run / fast *My sister can run faster than my brother.* _____

2 swim / quickly _____

3 write / well _____

4 work / hard _____

5 speak / clearly _____

③ Grammar reference

Lesson 3: Relative pronouns

1 Read and complete.

> that   when   where   which   ~~who~~

Relative pronouns		
She's the person	¹_____who_____	helped me.
A factory is a place	²_____	people make things.
What's the sport	³_____ / ⁴_____	you like best?
Spring is a time	⁵_____	flowers start to grow.

2 Read and complete the sentences with the words from the box and the correct relative pronouns.

> we know   I like   is tall   people do   ~~Tim gave~~

1 Anna lost the book _____*that Tim gave*_____ to her last week.

2 Evening is a time _____ to watch TV.

3 Jonathan is a boy _____ from school.

4 The gym is a place _____ exercise.

5 A tower is a building _____ and narrow.

Lesson 5: Past continuous

3 Read and complete with *was*, *wasn't*, *were* and *weren't*.

Past continuous				
I / He / She	¹✓_____was_____ / ²✗_____		sleeping	when the phone rang.
You / We / They	³✓_____ / ⁴✗_____			
What	⁵_____	he / she	doing	when the phone rang?
	⁶_____	you / we / they		

4 Read and complete the sentences with the Past continuous.

1 My teacher _____*wasn't running*_____ when I saw her in the park. (not/run)

2 Julia dropped her pen when she _____. (paint)

3 What _____ at Sam's house when I phoned? (you/do)

4 They _____ lunch when the bell rang. (not/have)

5 It started to rain when my friends and I _____ football. (play)

6 What _____ yesterday when you saw him in the library? (he/read)

Lesson 3: Present perfect with *already, just* and *yet*

1 Read and complete.

has   hasn't   have   haven't   's   ~~'ve~~

Present perfect with *already, just* and *yet*		
I ¹'ve_____ You've He's / She ²_____ We've / They've	already	had breakfast. tidied the kitchen.
	just	finished the project. swept the floor.
I ³_____ He / She ⁴_____	had breakfast tidied the kitchen	yet.
⁵_____ you	finished the project	yet?
⁶_____ anyone	swept the floor	

2 Write sentences about your day. Use the Present perfect with *already, just* or *yet*.

1 tidy my room _____

2 write a sentence _____

3 chat with my friends _____

4 have dinner _____

5 watch TV _____

Lesson 5: Sense verbs: *look, smell, taste, sound, feel*

3 Read and complete.

tastes   ~~does~~   it   like   feels   smell   looks   sound

Sense verbs: *look, smell, taste, sound, feel*		
What ¹____does____ it	look / ²_____ / taste / ³_____ / feel	⁴_____?
⁵_____	⁶_____ / smells / ⁷_____ / sounds / ⁸_____	good / bad / soft / lovely. like (water) / like a / an ...

4 Read and complete the sentences with the correct form of the sense verbs.

1 This ice cream ____tastes____ like strawberrries.

2 Those houses _____ really new.

3 This shampoo _____ like lemons.

4 That _____ like classical music.

5 Ouch! These shoes _____ too small.

Lesson 3: *too* and *not ... enough*

1 **Read and complete.**

isn't   enough   ~~is~~   too   are

too and *not ... enough*			
This jacket	1 ___*is*___	3 _____	casual. boring.
These shoes	2 _____		
This dress	4 _____	smart tight	5 _____ .
These jeans	aren't		

2 **Write sentences using the words in brackets and *too* or *not ... enough*.**

1 These shoes are too small. (big)   *These shoes aren't big enough.*

2 My jeans aren't tight enough. (baggy)   _____

3 This belt is too short. (long)   _____

4 The weather isn't warm enough. (cold)   _____

5 Those leggings are too casual. (smart)   _____

6 This shirt isn't new enough. (old)   _____

Lesson 5: Present passive

3 **Read and complete.**

~~called~~   used to   leather   kings   used for

Present passive		
It's	1 ___*called*___	silk.
	made of	2 _____ .
	3 _____	make shoes.
They're	4 _____	making clothes.
	worn by	5 _____ .

4 **Read and complete the sentences with the Present passive.**

Cotton balls ¹___*are picked*___ (pick) from cotton plants. Then they
²_____ (send) to factories. They ³_____ (clean) by machines. The
cotton ⁴_____ (make) into blue cloth. This cloth ⁵_____ (call) denim.
The denim ⁶_____ (use) for making jeans and jackets. Denim jeans and jackets
⁷_____ (wear) by people all around the world.

Lesson 3: Indefinite pronouns

1 Read and complete.

> anyone   anything   anywhere   everywhere   no one   nothing   ~~someone~~

Indefinite pronouns			
	one	**thing**	**where**
some	1 ___Someone___ called you.	I found something.	I went somewhere.
any	Did 2 _____ call you? There wasn't anyone.	I didn't find 4 _____ . There wasn't anything.	I didn't go anywhere. There isn't 6 _____ to go.
no	3 _____ called you.	There was 5 _____ .	There's nowhere to go.
every	Everyone called you.	I found everything.	I've been 7 _____ .

2 Read and circle the correct answers.

1 I don't think … will go camping.

   a no one   **b** anyone   **c** someone

2 We should go … fun tomorrow.

   a anywhere   **b** nowhere   **c** somewhere

3 Please put … into that big box.

   a everything **b** nothing   **c** anything

4 There's … we can do about the problem.

   a nowhere   **b** no one   **c** nothing

5 I need … to help me tidy the house.

   a someone   **b** anyone   **c** no one

6 We can't go … right now. It's raining.

   a everywhere **b** anywhere   **c** nowhere

Lesson 5: *should/shouldn't, must/mustn't, need to/don't need to*

3 Read and complete.

should/shouldn't, must/mustn't, need to / don't need to		
I You He / She We They	1 ___should___	eat healthy food.
	shouldn't	eat too much chocolate.
	must	be on time.
	2 _____	be late for Maths.
	need to / 3 _____ to	see a doctor.
	don't / 4 _____ need to	wear a uniform.

4 Write sentences about you and people you know. Use your own ideas.

1 I / should   ✗ *I shouldn't go to bed late on week nights.* _____

2 My friends / must   ✓ _____

3 Everyone / need   ✓ _____

4 Our teacher / should   ✓ _____

5 I / must   ✗ _____

6 Children / need   ✗ _____

7 Grammar reference

Lesson 3: Present perfect with *since* and *for*

1 Read and complete.

for   has   I've   ~~long~~   year   lived   weeks

Present perfect with *since* and *for*			
How ¹ _____long_____	have you ² _____ he / she		been a singer? lived in London? had a phone?
³ _____ He's / She's	been a singer ⁴ _____ in London had a phone	since	nine o'clock. last ⁵ _____. I / he / she was a baby. this morning.
		⁶ _____	three days. two ⁷ _____. five months. a long time.

2 Read and complete the questions with the Present perfect. Complete the answers with *since* or *for*.

~~be~~   know   live   study

1 A: How long __*have*__ you __*been*__ a student?

B: __*Since*__ I was five years old.

2 A: How long _____ you _____ here?

B: _____ about six months.

3 A: How long _____ you _____ English?

B: _____ three or four years.

4 A: How long _____ you _____ your teacher?

B: _____ last September.

Lesson 5: Present continuous for future arrangements

3 Read and complete.

having   next   playing   this   ~~we're~~

Present continuous for future arrangements		
I'm ¹ _We're_ They aren't	going to the cinema ² _____ a party seeing friends ³ _____ football	⁴ _____ afternoon/evening. tonight/tomorrow. ⁵ _____ week/month. on Saturday.

4 Write sentences that are true for you.

1 I'm playing tennis next Saturday.   _I'm playing basketball next Saturday._

2 My friends are ice skating tomorrow. _____

3 Our school's closing for the holiday. _____

4 I'm having a party this evening. _____

5 My family's visiting Paris this year. _____

Lesson 3: *may, might, could, can't, must*

1 **Read and complete.**

can't	could	~~may~~	must	might

may, might, could, can't, must			
It	might / ¹ _____*may*_____ / could	be	a fish.
	² _____ / can't	have	fins.
You / He / She	³ _____ / may / ⁴_____	be	correct.
	must / ⁵_____		serious.

2 **Read and complete the sentences with *may, might, could, can't* and *must*. Use each word once.**

1 That little animal _____*may*_____ be a hedgehog. It has long spines.

2 The girl next to the window _____ be Sarah, but I'm not sure.

3 This red jacket _____ belong to Sam. He was wearing it today.

4 Paul doesn't look very interested in the film. He _____ be bored.

5 You _____ be hungry now. You ate a big lunch an hour ago!

Lesson 5: First conditional: *if ..., ... will ...*

3 **Read and complete.**

die	~~have~~	not/be	not/disappear

First conditional: *if ..., ... will ...*	
If you go to the zoo with me,	we ¹ _____*will have*_____ lots of fun.
If we protect our forests,	they ² _____ .
If we don't water the plants,	some of them ³ _____ .
If I forget to do my homework,	my teacher ⁴_____ happy.

4 **Read and complete.**

1 If I see an animal in the forest, I _____*will take*_____ (take) some photos.

2 If we leave soon, we _____ (not/be) late for dinner.

3 If you help me to study for the test, I _____ (buy) you lunch.

4 If we give food to bears, they _____ (become) a problem.

5 If Ben tidies his room, his mum _____ (not/be) angry with him.

6 If they visit the palace, they _____ (see) the king and queen.

9 Grammar reference

Lesson 3: *going to* and *will*

1 **Read and complete.**

going to and *will*		
I ¹ _'m_____ You ² _____ We ³ _____	going to	travel by plane. ⁴ _____ an umbrella.
I He She	'll ⁵ _____	help you with that. ⁶ _____ to the museum. take lots of photos.

go
'm̶
aren't
're
take
won't

2 **Read and complete the dialogues with the verbs in brackets and *going to* or *will*.**

1 **A:** Why did you buy so many eggs?

    B: I _____ (make) a cake.

2 **A:** Oh, no! It's raining. We can't go out.

    B: Then we _____ (watch) TV.

3 **A:** Do you have plans with Suzy?

    B: No, we _____ (not/go) out.

4 **A:** You have to meet me at five o'clock.

    B: OK. I _____ (not/be) late.

5 **A:** Why is Ben looking in the shoe shop window?

    B: He _____ (buy) some new trainers.

6 **A:** The kitchen floor is a mess!

    B: Don't worry. I _____ (sweep) the floor.

Lesson 5: Present simple for the future

3 **Read and complete.**

Present simple for the future		
The plane The ¹ _train___	leaves ² _____ lands	in 15 minutes. at six o'clock. in two hours.
What ³ _____ When	does ⁴ _____	the plane ⁵ _____ off? the tour ⁶ _____ ? we catch the train?

arrives
at
start
take
time
tra̶i̶n̶

4 **Look, read and complete the travel itinerary with the Present simple for the future.**

arrive   have   l̶e̶a̶v̶e̶   take off   explore   land   catch a bus

1 We _____ _leave____ home tomorrow morning at 8.00 am.

2 The plane _____ from London Gatwick airport at 11.30 am.

3 The flight _____ in Paris at 1.00 pm.

4 We _____ from the airport to the city centre at 2.00 pm.

5 We _____ at the hotel at 3.00 pm.

6 We _____ the city at 3.30 pm.

7 We _____ dinner in a restaurant in the city at 8.00 pm.

Wordlist

Starter

Physical appearance

handsome

medium-height

pretty

short

tall

Personality adjectives

bossy

brave

chatty

clever

creative

energetic

friendly

fun

kind

noisy

Unit 1

Sports

do athletics

do gymnastics

do yoga

go cycling

go ice skating

go scooting

go skiing

go snowboarding

play badminton

play hockey

play table tennis

play volleyball

Hobbies

collect cards

do photography

do puzzles

do the gardening

go to concerts

make models

make videos

play musical instruments

put on shows

sing in a choir

watch cartoons

write a diary

W Wordlist

Unit 2

Devices

app	_____
devices	_____
digital camera	_____
earphones	_____
e-reader	_____
laptop	_____
password	_____
printer	_____
screen	_____
smartphone	_____
speaker	_____
website	_____

Using technology

click on an icon	_____
download an app	_____
go online	_____
press a button	_____
search the internet	_____
send a message	_____
take a selfie	_____
turn off the TV	_____
turn on the computer	_____
type a password	_____
upload a photo	_____
watch a video	_____

Unit 3

Places and buildings

apartment building	_____
castle	_____
factory	_____
harbour	_____
hospital	_____
office building	_____
palace	_____
skyscraper	_____
sports centre	_____
stadium	_____
swimming pool	_____
tower	_____

Parts of buildings

ceiling	_____
corner	_____
corridor	_____
entrance	_____
escalator	_____
exit	_____
floor	_____
lift	_____
roof	_____
stairs	_____
steps	_____
wall	_____

Unit 4

Chores

clear the table _____

cook the dinner _____

do the washing-up _____

dust the furniture _____

empty the bin _____

load the dishwasher _____

put away the clothes _____

sweep the floor _____

take the dog for a walk _____

tidy up _____

vacuum the carpet _____

water the plants _____

Food and drink

add _____

bake _____

boil _____

chop _____

chopsticks _____

cut _____

fork _____

knife _____

mix _____

pepper _____

salt _____

spoon _____

Unit 5

Describing clothes

baggy _____

casual _____

comfortable _____

fashionable _____

patterned _____

plain _____

smart _____

spotted _____

striped _____

tight _____

uncomfortable _____

unfashionable _____

Clothes and accessories

belt _____

bracelet _____

crown _____

earrings _____

gloves _____

leggings _____

sweatshirt _____

tie _____

tights _____

top _____

watch _____

woolly hat _____

Wordlist

Unit 6

Outdoor equipment

bandage _____

blanket _____

camping stove _____

compass _____

first-aid kit _____

matches _____

penknife _____

plaster _____

rope _____

rucksack _____

shelter _____

sleeping mat _____

Injuries and accidents

break your arm _____

burn your hand _____

call an ambulance _____

cut your finger _____

fall over _____

have a pain _____

have an accident _____

hurt your ankle _____

keep cool _____

keep warm _____

lie down _____

take medicine _____

Unit 7

Jobs in entertainment

acrobat _____

ballet dancer _____

camera operator _____

clown _____

comedian _____

composer _____

costume designer _____

ice skater _____

make-up artist _____

performer _____

presenter _____

writer _____

Places of entertainment

3D cinema _____

adventure playground _____

aquarium _____

art gallery _____

bowling alley _____

circus _____

concert hall _____

ice rink _____

planetarium _____

safari park _____

science museum _____

theme park _____

Unit 8

Animal body parts

antennae

beak

claws

fins

flippers

paws

pouch

scales

spines

tongue

webbed feet

whiskers

Animal behaviour verbs

bite

curl up

die

dig

dive

fight

fly away

hide

lay eggs

roar

run away

sting

Unit 9

Holiday equipment

charger

flip-flops

guidebook

medicines

passport

pillow

raincoat

soap

suitcase

toothbrush

umbrella

washbag

Transport verbs

arrive

catch a bus

explore

get off

get on

go on a journey

land

leave

pack your suitcase

take off

take your seat

travel by train

Irregular verbs

Cover the Past simple and Past participle columns and check what you remember!

Infinitive	Past simple		Past participle	
be	was/were		been	
break	broke		broken	
bring	brought		brought	
buy	bought		bought	
catch	caught		caught	
choose	chose		chosen	
come	came		come	
do	did		done	
draw	drew		drawn	
drink	drank		drunk	
drive	drove		driven	
eat	ate		eaten	
fall	fell		fallen	
feel	felt		felt	
find	found		found	
fly	flew		flown	
get	got		got	
give	gave		given	
go	went		gone/been	
have	had		had	
hear	heard		heard	
hold	held		held	
keep	kept		kept	
know	knew		known	

Infinitive	Past simple		Past participle	
learn	learned		learned	
let	let		let	
lose	lost		lost	
make	made		made	
meet	met		met	
pay	paid		paid	
put	put		put	
read	read		read	
ride	rode		ridden	
run	ran		run	
say	said		said	
see	saw		seen	
sell	sold		sold	
send	sent		sent	
sing	sang		sung	
sleep	slept		slept	
stand	stood		stood	
take	took		taken	
teach	taught		taught	
tell	told		told	
think	thought		thought	
throw	threw		thrown	
wear	wore		worn	
win	won		won	

Progress path

Read and write. Then tick (✓).

Starter Unit

I'm **short / tall**. I have **straight / curly** hair and **dark / blue** eyes. I'm **chatty / shy** and **quiet / noisy**.

Unit 1

I _____ every day.
I _____ once a week.

Unit 4

It looks _____.
It sounds _____.
It feels _____.

Unit 3

What were you doing at four o'clock yesterday afternoon?

_____

What were you doing at ten o'clock last night?

_____

Unit 2

He's pressing...
a a message. ☐
b a button. ☐
c a selfie. ☐

Unit 5

They're _____ and _____. They aren't _____

Unit 6

I can't find **nothing / anything / everywhere** to eat. I can see **someone / somewhere / anyone** over there.

Unit 7

How long have you been at your school?
I've _____ for _____ .
I've _____ since _____ .

Unit 8

If it rains tomorrow, _____ .
If it's sunny tomorrow, _____ .

Unit 9

I need to **pack / explore** my suitcase. We're **travelling / catching** a bus at 5 pm. The plane **takes off / gets on** at 7.30 pm.

Pearson Education Limited
KAO Two
KAO Park
Hockham Way,
Harlow, Essex,
CM17 9SR England
and Associated Companies throughout the world.

www.english.com/teamtogether

The publishers would like to thank Viv Lambert and Kirstie Grainger for their
contribution.

First published 2020
Fifth impression 2024

ISBN: 978-1-292-29261-8

Set in Fruitger Neue LT 11pt

Printed in Slovakia by Neografia

Acknowledgements:
The publishers would like to thank teachers from schools in Madrid, Spain,
Istanbul, Turkey and Ankara, Turkey for their feedback and comments during the
development of the materials.

Image Credit(s):

123RF.com: Aleksey Boldin 24, andreahast 29, bbtreesubmission 59,
dolgachov 25, 94, 106, Eric Isselee 97, Jacek Chabraszewski 4, Jaromír Chalabala
73, Jens Ickler 108, kiwar 38, Mark Bowden 17, 22, mch67 88, Midkhat Izmaylov
88, Natalia Sheinkin 16, olivier26 134, saphira 25, Sergey Novikov 36, serrnovik
60, Tatiana Popova 25, tonobalaguer 33, ymgerman 25, Yuliia Sonsedska 98,
Yuriy Kirsanov 97; **Alamy Stock Photo:** age fotostock 61, Andrew Duke 33,
Angela Hampton Picture Library 76, Anka Agency International 21, Auscape
International Pty Ltd 99, Brian Perry 9, Cavan Images 9, christian kober 85, dpa
picture alliance 99, Elena Elisseeva 60, Eyal Bartov 59, flowerphotos 65, Image
Source Plus 3, Myrleen Pearson 27, Nataliia Prokofyeva 110, Nathan King 85,
85, Olena Kachmar 71, Pawel Opaska 11, petographer 96, Porntep Lueangon
65, RubberBall 9, The National Trust Photolibrary 61, Tyler Olson 86, Visuals
Stock 21; **Getty Images:** 10'000 Hours 48, FatCamera 3, fstop123 10, Fuse 34,
Hill Street Studios 17, Jose Luis Pelaez Inc 6, 82, vitapix 42, 78, Yasser Chalid
20; **Pearson Education Ltd:** Antonio Marcos Díaz 2, 3, 5, 17, 29, 40, 43, 55,
67, 78, 81, 93, 105, 116, 134, 135, Jon Barlow 86; **Shutterstock.com:** Andy
Dean Photography 23, Anna_Pustynnikova 47, CandyBox Images 77, Creatista
10, Damian Ryszawy 99, EcoPrint 102, ER_09 87, Geza Farkas 99, Golden Pixels
LLC 48, govindamadhava108 71, GRSI 59, Iakov Filimonov 97, Jia Li 109, littleny
67, margouillat photo 49, martellostudio 96, Oleksiy Mark 25, Pablo77 134,
Paul Looyen 100, paulrommer 96, PeanutsNSoda 102, Seasontime 135, Subin
Pumsom 102, Svetography 79, Thongchai S 72, V. J. Matthew 85, You can more
25

Illustrated by José Rubio, Juan Fender, Miguel Calero, Pablo Torrecilla, Oscar
Herrero, Pep Brocal, Christos Skaltsas (Hyphen) and Zacharias Papadopoulos
(Hyphen)

Cover Image: Antonio Marcos Díaz